You are the Style!

An Every Girl's Guide to Getting Dressed, Building
Confidence, & Shining from the Inside Out

LAURIE BRUCKER AMERIKANER

Illustrations by Amelia Noyes

Indigo River Publishing
3 West Garden Street, Ste. 718
Pensacola, FL 32502
www.indigoriverpublishing.com

You Are the Style: An Every Girl's Guide to Getting Dressed, Building Confidence, and Shining from the Inside Out | Laurie Brucker Amerikaner, author
ISBN 978-1-954676-00-8 | LCCN 2021903522

Edited by Tanner Chau
Cover and interior design by Emma Grace
Brand emblems by Jessica Krewson
Illustrations by Amelia Noyes

Special discounts are available on quantity purchases by corporations, associations, and others.
For details, contact the publisher at the address above.
Orders by US trade bookstores and wholesalers: please contact the publisher at the address above.

With Indigo River Publishing, you can always expect great books, strong voices, and meaningful messages.

Most importantly, you'll always find . . . words worth reading.

You are the Style!

This book is dedicated to my son, Ezra.
He is the heartbeat of everything that I do.

contents

PART I: STEP INTO STYLEPOWERMENT

PART II: FACE YOURSELF, THEN LOVE YOURSELF

PART III: THE STYLE SURVIVAL GUIDE

PART IV: SHINING FROM THE INSIDE OUT

acknowledgments

Words cannot express my gratitude for the love and support I have had through this journey of writing a book. Thank you to my parents, Vida and Alex Brucker, who, no matter what, have not just stood by my side but lifted me up, advised me, supported me, believed in me, and pushed me to be my best me every step of the way. The time we shared together over this process is something I cherish as it not only fills me with such love, but it added so much more love to my book. Thank you to my editor Tanner Chau, who from day one has been my cheerleader, coach, and voice of clarity. Even when I had my baby in the middle of the writing process, she allowed me the grace and space to heal and consistently supported me until the end. (And look what we did! High five!) Thank you to my Illustrator Amelia Noyes. I am so grateful for your creative whimsy, artistic style and inclusive vision to help draw my book alive.

And a final thank-you to my husband, Mike, who allowed me to put my heart and soul into this book, while holding our family unit together. I wrote this book newly pregnant, rewrote this book in my third trimester, and rewrote this book yet again as a first-time mom. Through the ups and downs of life, pregnancy, and new motherhood, Mike gave me the space, the compassion, the encouragement, and the motivation to keep going, loving me unconditionally through it all.

preface

We are living in unprecedented times. Throughout the year 2020, I've sat with a completed book. When our country shut down due to COVID-19, I questioned the relevance of this book. People lost paychecks, jobs, homes, and family members. How could I release a book about clothing and style when people were hurting so deeply? When the civil rights revolution came swinging back to the forefront of our society, I questioned the relevance of my book again. How can I share and promote my new book when there are seemingly more important issues we have to address? I've struggled with this questioning for months. However, as time carried on, I found new meaning in my life and in my book, transforming myself into a stylist *and* an activist.

My work as an activist has brought so much more meaning into my life and also helped shine a light on the deeper meanings inside *You Are the Style*. As you'll notice throughout the book, I touch upon spirituality here and there, as I have always seen style as being connected in some way. But in the past year my spiritual journey went from always seeking to deeply understanding and knowing. Throughout that transformation, here is what I reiterated to myself: *Change doesn't come from what is happening around us. Change comes from within us.* And remembering this truth was when the puzzle pieces came back together for me. I was looking for answers outside of me, when the answers were hidden inside of me.

You will quickly notice that this isn't a book about how to wear a specific item or dress on trend. This book will become a life manual to stepping into your own personal power. Getting dressed is not about the clothing, it's about you. It's about taking the deepest, hardest look at your own personal perceptions to discover what is truly underneath it all. The woman who can change it all. The woman of strength. The woman who can walk through the fire. The woman who can be the guiding light force in her own life, as well as in the lives of others.

That is why this book matters. Now more than ever. We as women can do our part every single day to create the world we want to not just see but live in. For ourselves, for children, for generations to come. We can lead the way! And no matter what the future brings, there is one thing that will repeat itself, over and over and over again, every day: you need to get dressed. Getting dressed each day is an energetic magic you bring to your own life as well as the lives of the people you come in contact with. By expressing your style, you are using one of the most powerful tools in your tool belt—the power to step into your best self in any given moment. Ready? Let's go.

author's note

In my work as a personal stylist for the past decade and change, I have met, styled, and connected with many incredible, resilient, inspiring, and dynamic women. Their stories have touched my soul and inspire me daily. They are why I do what I do. For the purposes of *You Are the Style*, I have modified names, narratives, and details in consideration of my clients' privacy and personal journeys.

Our individual style stories are so personal, and this book is filled with advice and experiences that are meant to inspire you to look at your own style journey through a new lens, while maintaining a level of continued privacy for my clients.

introduction

Have you ever felt like you were meant to do *something*? Something much more than where you feel stuck? Do you often wonder whether there is more to life than the one you are living?

Oh yeah—I know that feeling too. I mean, I always knew I was meant to do something big, and I had no idea what it was. But whatever *it* was, it would change the world. However, this little girl with big dreams also had deep, raging insecurities. I wasn't good enough. I wasn't pretty enough. I wasn't tall enough. I wasn't skinny enough. I wasn't cool enough. And I replayed these words over and over again in my head. I let those words stop me from reaching higher. I let those words infiltrate my system. And eventually I let those words be my reality, believing they were true for most of my life.

As the years went by, I walked the thin line of a double identity. On the outside I was a confident, colorfully stylish, badass entrepreneur; but on the inside I was an insecure, personally hypercritical young woman debilitated by my own doing. It was from this fine line I walked that I found my higher purpose: to share the tool that I used day in and day out to change the course of my life.

It's called *Stylepowerment. Oh, you've never heard of that before?* Well, that's because I made it up! So, let's break it down and make it part of your vocabulary:

Stylepowerment (noun)

Sty-le-pow-er-ment | \ ˈstī(-ə)l -ˈpau̇(-ə)r-mənt

Definition:

1) the confidence, conviction, and self-assurance created for oneself through defining, accepting, and owning one's individual style self-expression

2) to feel personal empowerment by wearing one's unique style unapologetically

Stylepowerment is the big magic I bring to the world. My higher purpose. My passion. My vision for all women. I live and breathe its possibilities every day. Stylepowerment is the core concept that has pulled me out of dark days over and over again as I navigate the continuous evolution of life. It lifts me up when I am down, empowers me when I am insecure, and emboldens me when I am less than confident. Over the years, using Stylepowerment as my north star, my style journey has become a living, breathing representation of my personal empowerment story—my style{powerment} story, if you will.

Hey! You have one too! And we are going to write it together, starting today.

When I wrote the first draft of this book, I had an entirely different introduction. A story of Laurie, living it up in New York City, styled to the nines on the daily, and a walking shell of a woman. On the outside I projected all that was fabulous about fashion, style, and expression, but on the inside I was miserable. I used my wardrobe as my protective armor to fend off the insecurities and distract from the self-deprecating mind games.

But a spiritual awakening occurred while I was working through revisions with my editor that opened my eyes. There was something bigger going on here than just my story of style survival in the fast fashion wilderness. The real story was one of self-worth. And it wasn't just the introduction story. It was the story I wrote in one chapter about trying to be like all the other girls in college. It was my story I wrote in another chapter about trying to dress like the other girls in New York. It was my story in a different chapter about the loss of my self-confidence striving to be somebody I was not. While each story had its own twists and turns, fashion faux pas and style successes, they all came down to the same underlying lesson and ultimately my life-changing realization.

My whole life I have been striving to feel validated by other people and worthy, doing everything in my power to dress like I fit in . . . only to discover that I stand out.

Each time, as I tried to go against who I am to find acceptance and approval from others, I was just cutting deeper into the invisible wound I kept reopening over and over again: *I am not worthy*. And if "they" can't accept me, then I must not be good enough.

Oh, the irony of trying to fit in only to stand out. Over time, standing out became the style story I shared with the world. If I couldn't be accepted, then I was going to define my own acceptance and dress in a way that made me feel like I was creating my own energy movement around me. Having repeated this history, using Stylepowerment to continuously lift me up, a new gear shifted when I had my first child. A realization that rocked my world and changed me *forever.*

I have always looked to others to define my self-worth. And in admitting that to myself, I can only respond with such powerful conviction: They don't define my worth—I DO!

Then it all hit me. My wardrobe is a love story for my own self-worth, yet I didn't have my eyes open to see it that way. I was viewing myself in a negative light, and the world around me felt down, dark, and difficult to navigate. But when I dressed to feel like my most powerful self, I could see (and feel!) my strength, my beauty, and my unique soul essence. I could then use that energy to fuel and empower me into a higher level of living. In the beginning I may have used my wardrobe as armor against the world, but in reality, my wardrobe was my personal liberation.

At the core, how we feel and what we wear to reflect our feelings are contributing factors to the energy we put out into the world. Don't feel good in your clothes? It shows. Not just physically but energetically. Feel incredible in your clothes, it not only shows, it shines beyond your outfit into the outside world. It's essentially the powerful Law of Attraction at work! For me, Stylepowerment is the art of living your life at a higher vibration by utilizing your clothing, your style, and your fully self-expressed energy as a manifestation portal. Your wardrobe thus becomes a creative tool for you to create your own uniquely inspired and desired life.

The one thing I've learned over the years and continue to relearn over and over again (*Thanks, life!*) is that our lives are all about perspective. It's like we tether ourselves to a version of our story that isn't necessarily the reality of what is around us. How we see our world is how we in turn view ourselves and our style. When everything feels like it's falling apart, your closet becomes a dark, cavernous hole of despair and insecurity. When everything feels like it's all working in your favor and life is bright, your closet and your life feel like a place of powerful possibility.

But let's flip that script because it is just as powerful. When you view yourself and your style as something insecure, undeserving, and unworthy, the world around you feels heavy, weighted, and impossible. When you and your closet are in a place of creativity, inspiration, and love, the world around you opens up! Possibility is all around you, not just in your wardrobe but in all aspects of your life. And that is exactly what we are here to do!

No matter what you are going through, good or bad, you have to get dressed. Each time you stand in front of your closet you get to make a decision for yourself. Is this outfit choice going to drain you or fuel you? Is this outfit going to stay in the low vibrational level that supports the negative stories you tell yourself? Or is this outfit going to bring you to a place of high vibration, empowerment, and confidence? I've personally experienced both.

I've had bad days when I've gotten up and instead of putting on an outfit that was ever so stylish, I succumbed to my morning mood, picking out an outfit that matched my mental state and low vibe after throwing all the contents of my closet on to the floor. *Those are fun mornings, aren't they?* I've also had days when I get up feeling so excited to put on an outfit that is going to make me feel like my most fabulous me, and I pull out the perfect outfit combination on the first try! Such a difference that day is and such a difference *I feel.*

So, the question is, can we use our wardrobe to change our perspective of ourselves and the world around us? Can we utilize wardrobe as a tool to get us out of our heads and bring us to see the world with optimism and limitless opportunity?

I believe we can.

I know we can.

I've manifested this kind of life for myself, and I've worked one-on-one with women for over a decade to teach them how to do the same. And guess what? I'm going to teach you, as well, to break free from those mindset barriers and break into your most confident, ever-stylish, effortlessly self-expressed YOU.

EMPOWERING WOMEN, EMPOWERING MYSELF

There is this moment, a split second in time, when it all clicks. The clouds part, a bright light shines from above, a melodic harmony of "*aaaaahhhhh*" surrounds you, and the gates open up right before your eyes. It is the moment when I turn my client to the mirror and she finally sees what I see. That she is beautiful. That she is powerful. That she is feminine. That she is a work of art, no matter her shape, color, or size. That her own Stylepowerment is possible! And then the tears come.

We both cry. Let's be honest: I'm a total sap. Seeing my clients make this powerful shift in their personal perception is literally the reason I do what I do and teach what I teach.

For me, this journey to deliver Stylepowerment to all women started with just one closet. One woman. One session. Over the course of my styling career, I've worked with CEOs, girl-bosses, entrepreneurs, working moms, stay-at-home moms, divorcées, widows, musicians, actors, and more. Each and every one was experiencing all the twists life has to offer, but all ended up in the same place: disconnected from themselves and their heart-center. Their lives, their bodies, and their priorities were different than they once were. When all of these things catch up to us, we lose sight of ourselves and, in some cases, give up entirely. Our style can wait until everything else is done first. Our self-care is last on the list after handling the family or household to-do list. Shopping for ourselves happens after all the shopping for the kids is done. Our closets accumulate more unworn pieces and collect dust. It's that feeling of a point of no return when I step in.

In the years that I've worked directly with women, I have seen every possible way of giving up, which leads to silent suffering. From deep-rooted guilt to feeling and internalizing the real inequities of society, from self-hatred to even body shaming. I did it too! We all do. There is an epidemic in society that has caused us women to look in the mirror and see imperfections and insecurities, instead of seeing our most powerful selves. It breaks my heart. Particularly because my work made me realize what I was doing to myself day in and day out: expecting perfection from myself no matter the moment. From my clients, I learned I wasn't alone.

When you're feeling like there is no way out, I want to be there to show you a new way, to offer you a new perspective, to put out a hand and let you know you are not alone—and you don't have to go through this alone. The truth is we are all so different and so beautiful in our own ways. My work is more than the clothes. It's self-help through style. It's the utilization of your clothes in a way that supports you, your life, and your soul purpose. Your style is the ultimate act of self-care, and when you truly own that style creation you unlock your boundless confidence tucked away inside.

My work as a personal stylist and empowerment coach has only strengthened my duty to give you the opportunity to see yourself and the world around you in an entirely fresh, new light. Inside these pages you will get more specifics, details, advice, anecdotes, and inspiring client transformation stories. You will learn how to rewrite your own style story. I will teach you how to paint your own style expression and continue to design a life that always inspires you. You will learn not only to find Stylepowerment within yourself but how to cultivate it, to embrace it, to live it, and to *be* it.

Women are way more powerful than we could ever imagine. We are strong, resilient, bright, magnificent, beautiful, imperfect, and absolutely perfect *just the way we are.* When you learn to embrace who you are, accept where you are, love who you are, and own that in your personal expression, you will discover that you ARE the style.

I can't wait to empower you. Let's get started.

PART I

step into stylepowerment

CHAPTER 1

throw out the fashion rules

PERMISSION SLIP

In my decade of styling, one thing has become very clear to me about women. We have accumulated *sooooooo* much information on what we are supposed to wear—too much information! As time carries on, we mature, our lives changes, our bodies change—everything changes! And *yet* those pesky rules, notions, nags, thoughts, insecurities, doubts, and fears that we have accumulated in our wardrobe over the years seem to pop up day after day, wreaking havoc on all of our creative minds.

When working with private clients, I get the same wide-eyed, jaw-to-the-floor reaction when I make simple statements like:

"Yes, you can wear black and brown together!"

"Of course you can wear white denim in the winter!"

"Absolutely! Your shoes and your handbag can be different colors."

"Go for it! You can one hundred percent have fun mixing your prints."

Or here's a personal favorite: "For sure! You can absolutely put a belt on that."

Over the years, we have all collected a Pandora's box of fashion rules, tips, guides, musts, must-nots, dos, don'ts, and everything in between. Those loving words of advice from our moms, our grandparents, our friends, our coworkers, and even our significant others stick with us. They're stored away in a not-so-stylish but easy-to-grab handbag ready to be pulled out at any given moment. Their main job is to complicate the art of getting dressed. I mean, how can you decide what to wear when you have thoughts like this dictating, clouding, and even blocking your creativity and self-expression?

Do these phrases sound familiar?

You can't wear black and navy together.

You should never wear any white after Labor Day.

You should always match your purse to your shoes.

You must wear a suit to look professional.

You can't mix those prints.

Silver and gold can't be worn together.

You should never wear horizontal stripes.

You can't wear your casual clothes and your dressy clothes together.

Black is the most slimming color. Always.

Sparkle is for the evening only.

If it still fits, you should definitely keep the piece.

A flashy necklace will draw too much attention.

Are you suuuure that blouse goes with those pants?

You can't wear that at your age.

You must wear this if you're pregnant.

You can do this.

You can't do that!

You should always do this.

You should never do that!

. . . and the list goes on!

So. Many. Rules. Our brains are holding on to so much information, we can't sort out what's "right" and what's "wrong." This mental chaos clogs our flow. Truthfully, this happens to all of us—including me! I can't tell you how many times I have stood in front of my closet only to say to myself, "Oh no, that doesn't work . . ." and then list some off-the-cuff rule that was ingrained in my mind. Instead of wearing what my heart desired, I chose something else to satisfy some so-called "rule" I was once told to conform to.

I bet you can think of a few more that relate directly to you. Keep them coming. I want you to pour everything out of your mind. From this moment forth, you have a blank canvas to paint when it comes to you, your body, and your style. This is a fresh start. An open perspective. An exciting new journey. With this blank slate, you get to rewrite your own Stylepowerment story. Not your mom's story, not your sister's story, not your great-auntie's story, not your friend's story, not your coworker's story. Your *own* story. It is a whole new story that you get to pen, design, and color exactly how you've always dreamed it to be.

Ready to find freedom in a single word? I give you **permission**! This is officially your permission slip!

Permission to let go, permission to start fresh, permission to give yourself a clean slate to work from. You get to redesign your future! One thing I've learned in life is that nothing is ever set in stone. For wherever we are in our lives, we are never stuck; we only think we are stuck. Our fears and insecurities tether us to this false belief. We can only see darkness when, in reality, it is in our nature to create the light. That is *this* moment. You have the ability to change your fate. Make strides toward your own light, dig deeper to find your heart-center, and lead from there. Find a path of self-expression that not only fuels you but makes you shine. THAT is the story you get to write.

YOU AREN'T THE FASHION

According to the Merriam-Webster dictionary, *fashion* is, by definition, "the prevailing style (as in a dress) during a particular time." An example would be "The spring fashions are now on display." True! That *is* fashion. In addition, the dictionary says *fashion* is also "a garment in such a style." The example here is "She always wears the latest fashions." Also true! Notice how they are articulating the singularity of the fashion by identifying its tangibility: "as in a dress" or "a garment," which is absolutely correct. Fashion is tangible! Fashion is material. But! Fashion is also fleeting. Here today, gone tomorrow. Thanks to the internet, we have seen a dramatic shift in the speed of fashion information that is bombarding us daily. What is hot and "in fashion" today is not necessarily what is "in fashion" next week.

Fashion is the actual physical items of wardrobe. The clothes, shoes, handbags, accessories, and everything currently in the height of their trending peaks are considered *fashion*. It's that gold sparkling gown walking down the runway. The mixed-print jumper by Alice and Oliva at Bloomingdale's.

The sculptural dress by Cushnie in the boutique down the street. From the runway to the real way, the *fashion* is in the actual items!

Think about it this way: *Fashion* is also what is IN our closet. It's that special-occasion dress hanging in your closet just waiting to be worn, it's your favorite jeans you picked up last season, it's the handbag collection you have amassed and the mountain of jewelry you never wear, tucked in your drawers. *Fashion* is also what you can find as the "must-haves" of the moment, whether you see it in magazines, on your favorite bloggers, in TV shows, on red carpets, on celebrity street style, or on E! News. Very simply, when you purchase a new dress, THAT is *fashion*.

Let me tell you about one of my clients. Gabrielle lived for fashion. She was lovingly supported by her family, so she could shop for whatever she desired. She bought anything and everything under the fashion sun that made her happy. When I first started working with her, Gabrielle had stuffed her huge closet to the brim, full of fashion. She filled the racks with studded jackets, long jackets, short jackets, frilly blouses, and edgy tops. Torn T-shirts, sexy bodysuits, pencil skirts, and miniskirts hung together in a posse. A whole section devoted to denim was color coordinated, the items folded over on their hangers. Boxes and boxes of high heels, cute flats, and funky boots stacked the shelves surrounding the closet. There were rows of shelves filled with handbags and clutches, big and small. Her crowded drawers were well over capacity with all kinds of jewelry, from glamorous to classic to bohemian. So. Much. *FASHION!*

With all that fashion in her closet, one might think our session together would be a breeze. But think again. I asked Gabrielle what she wore the most, and she pulled out an old, pilling printed-jersey-knit halter-top maxi dress.

"I basically wear this every day with my flip-flops," she said.

I'd like to tell you that my jaw dropped, but for as long as I have been styling, this has been a common closet experience. A closet full of fashion, yet nothing to wear. It's tragic!

I asked her why she didn't wear any of her other clothes.

"Because I don't know how to put anything else together. I know I like everything, but when I put it on, I just don't know what I'm doing. Do these pants go with this top? Does this skirt go with this jacket? I just don't know, so I give up and wear the same thing every day."

Like many of my clients, this scenario goes deeper than just not knowing how to put the clothes together. I can always tell when there is something more going on. As we worked through her wardrobe, she shared with me that her weight had fluctuated dramatically for years. No matter what her body looked like, Gabrielle always saw herself as imperfect. She bought clothes she loved, yet never felt good enough in her own skin to wear them. She didn't see how beautiful she already was.

To mask this secret struggle, she shopped for all the fabulous fashion she could get her hands on. Yet each purchase she made only brought her a small spark of joy while allowing her to suppress the deep-rooted insecurity she was holding on to. Not being able to wear all her fabulous clothes was a painful reminder, but not even knowing where to start led to Gabrielle giving up entirely. For all the clothes she bought, it was the *fashion* that made her happy, but it was also the fashion that inflicted the most pain.

They don't call shopping "instant gratification" for nothing! When we shop, our brains get a shot of dopamine and we say, "YAY! I feel happy! This is awesome!" When you bring home your new top, it gets put away in your closet. It hangs there until you finally try it on again, and you can't figure out what to wear with it. So the item takes its place in the depths of your closet, possibly never to be seen again. Yeah, we all have had *that* piece!

Shopping does not ultimately create our happiness, and neither does *fashion*. Trying to keep up with the fashion, the trends, and the seasons can leave you creatively exhausted. It's a distressing predicament to have a closet full of clothes and be utterly uncertain of what is really right for you. The good news is you don't have to be a servant to fashion anymore because you aren't the fashion. Not. At. All.

YOU ARE THE STYLE!

Now, what makes *style* different from *fashion*? *Style* is intangible! *Style* is determined by you. It is how you, as an individual, interpret all the fashion out there. It's how you take all the little bits of fashion information in and make them your own. You can't hold *style*. You can't touch it. Instead, you get to create it!

By definition (according to the Merriam-Webster dictionary) *style* is "a distinctive manner of expression," "a distinctive manner or custom of behaving or conducting oneself," or "a particular manner or technique by which something is done, created, or performed." Included definitions of *style* are "a state of being popular," as in "clothes that are always in style." These definitions all make sense, but the dictionary doesn't address *style* in its most profound form as it pertains to the individual, because *style* is so much more.

The good news for you is this whole book is about ***style***!

Style, in every possible sense, depth, and essence of the word, is not something you can touch. Instead, *style* is something you can feel, see, and even taste when it's good. Let's start with a simple breakdown of *style*. My friend and I own the same white V-neck tee. Now, she prefers a very simple and casual look. She wears the white tee with a pair of skinny jeans, suede peep-toe booties, and an oversized duster sweater with a pendant necklace. That's *her* style! When I wear my white V-neck tee, I pair it with a black lace pencil skirt (tucked in, of course) with a yellow leather motorcycle jacket, lace-up heels, and a bold necklace in coral. That's *my* style! Both are great outfits, both are right for us individually, and both make us feel great. This versatility is the beauty of *style*; it is different for everyone—and unique to you!

But! Wearing *fashion* in your own way isn't the full picture of what *style* is. It is also rooted in who you are and how you feel about yourself. Your style is *you*!

How many times has your mood dictated your outfit choice for the day? How about when you were feeling insecure, so you chose to wear something that made you feel more hidden? Or when you were feeling great about yourself and put on your favorite red dress, just because? What we are feeling at any given time can directly affect the choices we make when it comes to our style and self-expression, and vice versa.

One of the biggest challenges for my client Gabrielle as we continued our work together across multiple sessions was that she became so caught up in the *fashion*, she never understood her own ability for *style* and self-expression. What we discovered during our appointments together was that her deeper insecurities and feelings of body shame and the spiral of questioning how to put outfits together were actually dictating her choices about getting dressed in the morning. At the core, she wanted to try to wear the cool graphic tee, full pleated skirt, tan gladiator sandals, and a floppy hat. However, she was so stuck in her limiting beliefs about herself and her style that she didn't even allow herself to test it out in the first place. Her comfort zone kept her safe and sound in her old halter-top dress and flip-flops.

During our style session, Gabrielle and I worked on exactly how to put outfits together that made her feel creative, special, and beautiful. Using the science of *style*, we flattered her figure, played around with easy tools for getting dressed, and had a total blast while we did it. Together we started to tear down those barriers and comfort zones and replace them with opportunities and possibilities. Yes, she could try this skirt with that blouse or this pair of jeans with that jacket. The options were endless. Gabrielle saw herself, her closet, and her style in an entirely new light.

With a fresh set of eyes and an open mind, Gabrielle finally saw her true beauty beyond the wardrobe, and she began to embrace herself once again. This self-embrace turned into self-love, and that self-love was the spark that ignited her empowered style. Today she is living her life more fully, brightly, and confidently. She's making decisions in the morning that make her feel good. She's utilizing style techniques to try new things and get the most out of her closet and the clothes that made her happy. She is finally wearing her beautiful, fashionable wardrobe! And now she carries that feeling with her each and every time she heads out the door.

So do not fret. Even if you feel you have been stuck on *fashion*, you will be able to find freedom and liberation in *style*.

YOU DEFINE YOUR IMAGE

There is one more piece to the overall puzzle we must acknowledge as we embark on this journey together: your *image*. *Image*, different than *fashion* and *style*, isn't something personal to you or within you. Instead, *image* is outside of you. It is the visual perception of you. *Image* is how people see you and perceive you based on your *style* of self-expression. But don't let that scare you. Just because the perception is outside of you doesn't mean you don't control the message you get to send out to the world. Your style tells a story, and your *image* is the story that outside people perceive.

The concept of *image* will force you to dig deep. Let's take a hard look at your current style and current style choices; then I want you to answer this: What story are *you* telling about who you are? Does that style align with who you are? The notion can stop you in your tracks. It is even worth sitting down and having a meditative moment over it all. Here's why: when your style is misaligned with your desired message, that is the story people will read—the story about the woman you are not.

What about the story of the dynamic, smart, interesting, creative, powerful, brilliantly shining woman that you already are? Who's better and more equipped to tell her story than you? The good news is that you are not alone. So many women experience this, almost as if we unconsciously dim our own light, not even realizing the energetic consequences in our lives. Your image is the story you get to convey, and your style helps your story shine.

I tend to find that this conversation can bring up feelings and triggers in my clients. It can be painful to think that the way you've been dressing doesn't honor who you truly are. So if that strikes a chord for you, I want you to know *I get it*. I've been there too. Here's where it gets exciting! Considering how your image projects a message to others can be the next-level upgrade to your style and your life you've been asking for. Yep! Meditate for a minute on this: What will your life look like if your style aligned with the magic and message you bring to this world?

For Gabrielle, the image issue came up and brought some pretty major triggers with it. As we created each outfit, I would inquire, "When will you wear this next?" hoping to encourage her to take that big first leap into the world with her new style.

She would always reply, "I'm not sure," with such hesitancy.

As we kept hitting roadblock after roadblock, I finally was able to pull from her the underlying point of insecurity.

"But what will people think of me?"

And there you have it! Yet another thing to question in our Pandora's box of confusing thoughts and insecure talking points we say to ourselves as we get dressed. So yes, what will people think of you? That can be a terrifying notion, right? But this roadblock comes up often for women. "If I wear an outfit that feels like the true me, will other people judge me for it? Will I be accepted?"

How you project your style and your personal story is directly related to your self-worth. So many times we stop ourselves from wearing clothes that align with who we truly are for fear of what other people may think. Or we do it to fit in, or to hide in the background, or to stand out in a way that draws more side-eyes than positive attention. It's almost as if when getting dressed we decide to dull our true shine before we even walk out the door.

But that stops here. Right now, in this moment. This book is going to empower you with styling tools that will help you not just wear your clothes well but also to align with your message. The goal here is to teach you ways to pull out and point out all the different dimensions of you and your story. Style is not just one-sided, and your *image* is the opportunity to tell that multifaceted story of the woman that you are.

Having an awareness of your image and what it projects is a potent tool—kind of like a secret superpower to use when getting dressed. It's the power of intentionality. This is a concept near and dear to me. My very first tagline to my styling company, LaurieBstyle, was "Style Strategies for Success." To me, *style* is something to always be strategic about. *Style* is something you do on purpose. Having the tools to work with in your arsenal can be the small tweaks that become big game-changers for you in your life and career.

Image, like style, isn't something tangible. It's an outside perspective of your intangible style. Your image can also be used to support how you feel about yourself and how you see yourself in the mirror. Uplift that view of your beautiful self and imagine the possibilities! What makes you stylish, noticeable, magnetic, and head-turning is not something you can buy. Instead, it is something you get to cultivate, create, practice, build, and then get to live each and every day. You don't have to be "in fashion." Ever! You just get to be you, and that is the beauty of it all.

so, let's recap!

- Your permission slip is written! Take it to the streets and start fresh with a clean style slate to re-empower the new you.

- Fashion is tangible. It is all the physical clothes out there just waiting for you to interpret.

- Style is intangible. Style is self-expression! It is how you take the fashion and make it your own. Think about it as the intersection between fashion, image, and your inner spirit.

- Image is also intangible. It is how other people perceive you based on your style. It's also how you perceive yourself (i.e., self-image). Having an awareness of this sets you apart from the pack because it gives you the styling power of intentionality.

style statement

I give myself permission to become a blank palette for my own style expression by letting go of the rules that hold me back and being open to the possibilities to come.

the style mindset

LEAD WITH WHAT ELECTRIFIES YOU

"Fake it until you make it." It's one of those phrases we hear over and over again—in business, in life, and, yes, in style. But I see a deeper process than just faking it and making it. I see it as "fake it until you believe it, until you become it." Here's the super-duper secret: You already *were* it! YOU are the style! You've already got it all inside you. However, that is not the story we often tell ourselves.

Have you ever sat down and really thought about that? How you talk to yourself, what you say about yourself? *Oh, hey! Now is a great time *wink wink*.* What is the story you are telling *yourself* about you and your style? Not the story people see, but the story *you* see. You know, the one that re-plays again and again in your head. Here are a few examples that come to mind from my clients over the years:

You never had style.

You will never be stylish.

You don't deserve to be stylish.

Clothes never fit you.

You'll never find a dress that fits and flatters your midsection.

You never see yourself the way you want to feel.

You don't see yourself as beautiful. Or effervescent. Or colorful. Or sparkling. But you are just dying to be and don't know where on earth to begin with that kind of energetic transformation.

That narrative is a mighty force in your life. Your mindset about you and your style can determine not only the path you eventually take but the possibilities that will or won't open up for you as well. And a negative mindset will fuel the limitations you put up for yourself. Scary, right?

When we start to believe all these negative thoughts about ourselves, our lives, our bodies, and our style, we eventually begin to manifest our future exactly as we see it. We end up choosing an outfit in all dark colors or wearing that blousy fabric to hide our physical insecurities or dim our light. We continue to wear an old, worn wardrobe because we don't believe we deserve new clothing. Or how about this doozy: we feel like we gave up a long time ago and just submit to that mentality. It's crazy what negative views we can conjure up when we are in an unsupportive headspace.

But! What about those times when you felt powerful, positive, and dynamic? Remember those days? Everything felt open and full of opportunities! When the world felt like an exciting place to explore. When you *feel* that way your eyes, mind, and heart are open to see it. Your style is the same. Your style is all opportunities. It's everything you can fathom and imagine. When we've lost touch with that vision, we can lose sight altogether. Open yourself up to shift focus onto what possibilities you can create versus what you believe is possible. And yes, that is still possible, even now.

If you haven't noticed, this stylist is exceptionally spiritual. I'm all about looking within, connecting to the higher powers that be (whatever or whoever they may be for you), tapping into powerful vibrations, and manifesting your dreams across all areas of your life. And to me, your style is tied right into that manifestation. Because if you don't believe a stylish *you* is at all possible, then it's not. It's really that simple. If you just believe even a little bit of it is possible and really feel it, you will begin to see the power of creation you possess.

Ever try creating new neural pathways? *Okay, here we go—the science-y meets spiritual woo-woo stuff.* I'll never forget how I learned about the process, or at least a simplified one that was easy to chew on. Years ago, I had a client I took on a shopping trip for our style appointment. The whole time we were together, we were talking about life, love, and, of course, *style.* A week after our appointment I received a surprising email from her. She shared with me that she couldn't believe that I was still single, and she wanted to help me make space, energy, and change in my life to call in "The One." So she told me about this new tool she'd been studying for creating new neural pathways in the brain. Basically, it's the process of making new grooves in your brain to reshape your mindset and thinking.

She instructed me to sit and visualize my future husband and just feel that energy next to me. Then I was to say out loud, "I have the most amazing husband. He is loving, supportive, smart, handsome, and stable," and then rattle off all the other aspects about him and our incredible relationship. I was supposed to talk as if it had already happened and bask in the gratitude of that amazing feeling and experience. Part of me was like, *I have to say it out loud? I'm going to sound so ridiculous!* Even if the only one that could hear me was my cat, I just couldn't bring myself to do it!

Then one day in the car I thought, *Well, nobody can hear me in here, sooooo here we go!* And I sat there for twenty minutes talking to myself, bragging about the amazing man I had in my life, the way he made me feel, the life that we lived together, and on and on and on. I did it again and again and again. Saying it made it feel more real, feeling it made it seem more normal, and seeing my life in such a positive light became my destiny. The idea here was that this mindset I was creating for myself was not only making new grooves in my thought pattern but allowing me to really soak in and believe that this future was possible for me. (And yes, it all came true. More on that later.)

Personal style manifestation is the same in many ways. The more you change the story you tell yourself in your head, the more you are mindful of your mindset toward yourself and your style. By speaking powerful positive words, you speak your truth into reality. *Fake it until you believe it until you become it.* When you shift your mindset about yourself and your style, you begin to take actions that are more supportive of your vision, stepping into your Stylepowerment and making your empowered self second nature.

So, the big question remains, What does your highest self look like? Feel like? Sound like? Walk like? What is she wearing? Clearing your head of mental clutter is a surprisingly effective way to seek the answers you crave about who you are. The answers are within! I can say from personal experience that when I don't have a vision of who I want to be or how I want to express myself, I lose sight of myself, my path, and my life. Having that vision is an essential part of discovering your style. It will help you get some of those little sparks going as you step into the vision of the woman you want to be mixed with the embrace of the beautiful woman you already are.

It's important to explore what lights you up. Even if you are scared, not sure it will work, or just think it's totally outrageous. Allow yourself to explore your style without limitations. The key is to be open to possibilities, no matter what. Now is the time to lead with your heart and not your head. I mean, our heads just get in the way, right? What would your heart say if your head weren't already saying "NO, NO, NO" at every little flash of wild delight? Remember those rules we threw out the window? Well, tell them to stay out there! Your old beliefs about style are no longer needed. They have served their purpose, and your relationship with them is officially OVER. Your heart is officially in charge.

From now on, finding what electrifies you should lead you in your style exploration. Those jolts of excitement and adrenaline clue you in on what drives your heart. This is an excellent tactic for taking the lead in your life and supporting your stylish self-expression. For whatever excites you, here is the most important part: It's all good! Whatever it is! Don't hold yourself back. Don't stop yourself from something that you think might be perceived as weird or different. Just do what tickles your style soul. Try on clothes that excite you (and even make you a little nervous to carry into the dressing room). Put on that wild printed blouse! Wear those red heels! Top off your look with a hat! Just be you. But whatever you do, *don't stop yourself.*

EMBRACE YOURSELF

When it comes to style, before you learn the tools, it's mandatory that you deep dive into self-acceptance. Fully embracing yourself for who you are is just the magic you need to shine beyond your wardrobe. Self-acceptance means embracing everything about you: your body the way it is right now, your life the way it is right now, and *you* the way you are *right now*. For so many of us, we think we have to wait until something changes to take action. Reality check: waiting for change is what is holding you and your style back. Nothing positive comes if you are just waiting for something to change in order to feel good about who and where you are. You can feel good now! **You create the change!** You can take control by surrendering the things you can't change at this immediate moment, accepting them as they are, and finding love for the purpose they serve.

Let's be completely honest here: the process of learning to accept yourself can be daunting, and it is extremely personal. There really is no one way to cultivate self-acceptance. And it's not as if I am going to snap my fingers and, *poof*, you are going to jump out of bed tomorrow feeling different (although that would be nice, wouldn't it?). Accepting who you are and embracing yourself fully requires love, time, and a little (or a lot of) patience. Not every day is going to be perfect. Not every outfit is going to nail it. Through practice and consistency, you'll gain the ability to shift that energy habit into a whole new vibration. If you are truly going to rock your most confident style, you are first going to have to embrace your most beautiful self, from the inside out. Just the way you are. Right now.

Breaking news flash! At this very moment, you are precisely where you need to be in your life. Reading this book! Obvi! But in all seriousness, this is you right here, right now. *This* is your life. *This* is your body. *This* is where you are and what you've been through. Everything that has led you up to this point, good or bad. Through love and pain. Through joy and sadness. That is your story. That is your journey. You cannot change the past. All you can do is acknowledge it, surrender to it, accept that it happened, and set it behind you. That is the key to self-acceptance. A total, undeniable, and unrelenting embrace of who you are, inside and out. Sounds easy, right? Nope!

I can't even tell you how many times I have found myself in a state of despair over a feeling or memory that gets triggered and decides to linger. The worst is when I allow those feelings, those words, or those past mistakes to define who I see myself as today. It's as if all the incredible, powerful, and positive things that I have done are wiped away, overshadowed with the feeling of being diminished by my own demons. I have also seen it time and time again with my clients. They allow all of their perceived flaws to dictate their view of the world and of themselves. That perception affects their style choices.

My client Michelle was a perfect example of what happens when someone allows insecurities, demons, and negative notions to rule over their life and style. Michelle was affected by ageism, not just from societal norms but from her own misconceptions about age. Unfortunately, I see this a lot in women. How you view yourself in the mirror matters! The idea that once you hit a certain age you are outdated, old news, or undesirable is officially an obsolete concept and mentality. Whether it's an age that society says is "old" or what your internal voice says back to you in the mirror, this idea of ageism in our modern day can be an absolute determent to your soul fire and to your style. It's about time we prove this negative notion for women entirely wrong. Just because you are at any particular age, that shouldn't dictate anything about you—your beauty, your worth, your quality, or the power that you can bring to the table.

Michelle felt like she had been dealt the short stick. While her career flourished, having made partner in her law firm, her outside life and sense of self diminished as time carried on. She was fifty years old and single. She literally told me she was an "old bag," to which I replied, "Not a chance!" But regardless of reality, or how anyone else saw her, it was how Michelle viewed herself that mattered most. What I saw when I first met Michelle was a vibrant woman, a beautiful face with perfect laugh lines, a curvy body with a waist hidden behind draped fabric, and so much potential for her to blossom from this point in her life. There was still so much time for her to thrive.

Michelle's view of herself led her to dress in a way that didn't at all align with the incredible woman that she was. Instead, it aligned with the woman she saw herself as: "old." Not only did Michelle think she looked old, but she also embraced *feeling* old. We all know the adage that age is just a number, but it is true. Fifty is fabulous (all ages are fabulous!), and I was determined to show her how to generate that same vibration for herself. To Michelle's detriment, her closet supported the skewed story she was telling herself, and it was affecting her self-expression and style choices significantly. What I saw was a closet full of dim and dusty colors, dated prints, and faded suits. Her silhouettes were shapeless or full coverage, and overall, her fashion choices were just simply old-fashioned. Michelle's style reflected who she believed herself to be, not how others saw her or her vision of what she wanted to be. But that was all about to change!

It's my belief that, no matter your age, you can style yourself empowered, timeless, sexy, and beautiful. All you have to do is choose pieces that make you FEEL that way, instead of wearing pieces that make you feel everything but. Surprisingly to Michelle (but not to me! I can always find style in a closet, big or small), there were some really powerful pieces hidden in the mix of her closet. She had a few shift dresses, a new blazer she had picked up but hadn't worn yet, and a pair of slim denim she was holding on to but not choosing to wear. I paired her slim denim with one of her flowing work blouses, and instead of leaving the blouse out, like she normally wore it to hide her midsection, I half tucked the blouse in and added a skinny belt to the belt loops. We popped on her new blazer and a simple flat. From her jewelry drawer, I pulled out a necklace a friend had given her that she loved but never wore because she didn't know what to do with it. And voila! A perfect and expressive topper to a timeless and modern look. And that's all it took for Michelle to have her moment. It really was that simple. To shake things up in Michelle's closet, we had to shake up the routine. As I helped Michelle create outfits that felt fresh, fun, and still age appropriate, I tasked her with only styling with her newest pieces for a full week. She had a small capsule we were able to create from her closet together, and that was all she could wear.

A week later I checked in to see how everything was going for Michelle and almost fell out of my chair when she told me how her week had gone in her new looks. Of course, the first few days were uncomfortable to work through as she took on her style challenge with heart. But as each day went by, each time she looked into the mirror, each time she received a new compliment from a coworker, a stranger, and, oh yeah, that handsome man in the supermarket who asked for her number, it gave Michelle the spark she needed to open her eyes, her mind, and her heart to see the power of her own sense of style and the magic of the world she could create around her. She was rewriting the story she told herself. Each day she chose something empowering to wear that reinforced her new story—that she was a beautiful, strong, sophisticated woman who had so much to offer this world and the vibrant energy to do just that.

We all have something. We all have our demons; we all have our perceived flaws that haunt us on the daily. We are imperfect creatures: mind, body, and soul. And guess what? That is O-KAY! Actually, to be *perfect* means you are perfect as you are, fabulous imperfections and all. Accept that! Surrender to it. Allow it all to be. It's there, it's you, and it's enough. Because regardless of this, we all want more for ourselves and for our lives.

We all have dreams, visions, passions, desires, needs, wants, and goals. And the question is, Are you stopping yourself from reaching those dreams and showing the world who you truly are?

Your wardrobe is a powerful tool for you to utilize in your life. Even if you only have that one perfect piece (for now) that makes you feel incredible when you put it on. Whether it is dressy or casual, just put it on and remind yourself that YOU are amazing! This is the simplest way to kick-start the empowering tools of style in your life. I'm writing this style survival manual to give you your power back. The power to take control at any moment by opening your closet doors, pulling out your personal confidence armor, and stepping into your best self. The more you push through that personal pain in an acknowledging, compassionate, and self-caring way, the stronger you will become at fighting off the self-inflicted forces stopping you.

Let's start right now. I want you to catch yourself. When you look in the mirror, instead of rattling off the negative thoughts you default to, I want you to say instead, "I'm beautiful, I am powerful, I am resilient, I am woman!" Throw in a "hear me roar!" too, if you feel so compelled. Lead your life with that expression and the world, your style, and your story will be anything you want to create.

GET UNCOMFORTABLE

What worked for Michelle (though it is way easier said than done) was the art of getting uncomfortable. I've read somewhere that it takes twenty-one days of undeviating action and effort to create a new habit in your life. It takes even longer to break one. Change is hard! And *soooo* uncomfortable. To do things differently and really make this newfound way of style work effectively for you is going to take all your strength. So I get the hesitancy and I get the fear.

This is one of my favorite parts of the process with my clients who are writing their Stylepowerment stories for the first time. It happens almost every time after we have a successful "shop the closet" style session together. We've built thirty-something outfits, and they are absolutely spectacular and ready to go rock, except for one halting issue. *Fear!* My clients will realize how overwhelming this potential change in their lives is and are seemingly scared of what could come of it. Putting themselves out there like that for the whole world to see feels uncomfortable and downright terrifying!

"What will people think of my new look? What will they say?"

So just as great big change is about to occur, our heads get in the way and we stop ourselves in our tracks before we can even reap the benefits of our newfound sense of self. *ABORT! ABORT!*

My solution to this is simple: you *have* to get uncomfortable. You have to! You have to break through that horrible, gut-curdling feeling you get when you step outside the cozy embrace of your comfort zone. You have to defy your fear and push through, even if you stay uncomfortable all day! Even if it is uncomfortable just putting a new style or look on. Or wearing a heel to work for the first time instead of your regular flats. Or wearing a color combination you've never tried before. You just have to do it!

Now, because I can't be in every home each morning to use my style powers to get you out the door in a new look, there is an easy trick you can use to help you break free of your personal barriers. All I request of my clients, and this is for you, too, as you embark on trying new ways to wear your wardrobe, is that they start with one outfit. Pick one new look, one new way of doing things, and then you've got to get yourself out the door. You have to take that first step over the threshold and into the world. The world will never get to see YOU if you don't make that initial stride for yourself. First-day jitters really get the best of people, which is why sometimes it's a negotiation to get them out the door in their new, confident look. You just have to try it once, see how you feel, then try it all over again the next day.

It only takes one compliment, just one, to change that attitude around. Sometimes people will notice that something is different, but not be able to put their finger on it. Others will notice that you are sporting a belt and how fabulous it looks. Some may compliment you on a unique necklace choice or how outstanding the color you are wearing looks on you! It just takes one, and it will help reverse your fear-based perspective into budding confidence and eventually an intrigue for more. Then you have to try it all again the next day.

But here's the cool part. If you can effectively push yourself out the door in a new look each day that makes you look fabulous and confident, even though on the inside you may be shaking in your heels, you've already won the battle. It's that persistent defiance of your comfort zone to embrace a more confident wardrobe and a more confident you that will be the magic in the making. The idea is that each day you go out uncomfortable—maybe snagging a compliment here, meeting that guy's eyes across the room there, having your work wife gush over how fantastic you look—you start building up a little bag of feel-good occurrences. They act as encouragement when you make another conscious decision to put on an outfit that makes you feel fantastic, creative, unique, self-expressed! Before you realize it, you've become comfortable in your new look and with yourself!

The secret to breaking through fear and embracing your fabulous self is to get really uncomfortable. Like, really, *really* uncomfortable. You have to get uncomfortable to get comfortable again! That's what I always say.

The more often you get uncomfortable, the more you become comfortable doing it. You have to build muscle memory and new neural pathways for pushing through that fear—something you strengthen day after day. With each day you decide to choose style for yourself, getting yourself dressed will become easier. The easier getting dressed becomes, the more vibrant mornings you will have. And the more vibrant mornings you have, just imagine what your days will feel like!

STYLE IS A CHOICE

Do you see what I am getting at here? Your style is a choice. It's a decision you get to make each and every morning. Are you going to honor your beautiful self? Are you going to take your personal style statement seriously? Are you going to show the world your best *you*? Are you going to take those few extra minutes to pop on some jewelry to top off your outfit? Are you going to take the time to buckle up the heels that take forever to put on but when you wear them you feel like a goddess? Are you going to give yourself the opportunity to wear something that makes you shine? Those are serious questions. Yes, you can choose to revert to an old, easy style routine that doesn't serve you. Yes, you can choose to rush through getting dressed and not pay attention to the details. You can choose to assume everything will look bad and just wear that same piece you wear every time. You choose.

You are also choosing the kind of morning you will have. Will getting dressed feel like a drag? Or will it be inspiring? Will you be too tired to try? Or will you push through and put on something to perk up your mood? Will you wear that same black top? Or will you reach for the printed one you have been saving for a special day? Your style is YOUR choice. Now, as you continue to learn all the tools to support your style, will you choose to embrace this new way of thinking?

As you know, *style* isn't just about your clothing, *style* is a mindset. Style does not just come from within; it truly starts from within your mind. Style is what you set your mind to. Style is how you set up your mind for success. Style is your ultimate act of self-care. Style is your outward reflection of how you feel on the inside. Style is *your* choice, *your* chance to dress your best you every day and step into your Stylepowerment. Don't deny yourself that opportunity! Embrace it!

Let's make a pledge together:

"Today and every day after, I (your name here) will honor myself by making a conscious effort to style myself in a way that makes me feel fabulous, beautiful, and confident. No more will I wear things that don't feel good or serve my best self, and most importantly, no longer will I hide behind my clothes. Instead, I choose to take a chance, I choose to be a little uncomfortable, I choose to take action, and I choose style!"

This is the style mindset! Remember, fake it until you believe it, until you become it. Every day that goes by that you are not stepping into your own Stylepowerment is another day lost to an old mindset and an outdated version of you. Tomorrow is always a new day. So will you choose tomorrow to make one small change? One tiny outfit update that makes you smile. One mini mindset shift that will affect your whole day in a positive way. It's entirely up to you, and that's the beauty of it. There should be no guilt for where you are at this point. The amazing news is that you get to start tomorrow—heck, right now! And each day you get to do it again. Do you need to be perfect every day? No way! Like all self-work that we do to empower ourselves, it is a practice, meaning start where you are and grow from there. If you fall behind, then pick yourself back up and try again. The future version of yourself who gets dressed, owns her confidence, and shines from the inside out is just waiting for you to step into alignment with her!

so, let's recap!

- Lead with what electrifies you. Openness to opportunity is the catalyst for possibility in your life!

- Embracing yourself is vital to your style. Know that wherever you are at this very moment in your life, career, style journey, etc., it is the perfect jumping-off point for your personal transformation.

- Get uncomfortable! Change is so hard, but the more you make small strides, the bigger and longer lasting the impact will be over time.

- Style is your choice. With style as a mindset, you officially have the power to create the positive changes you want to see in your life. And it all starts with choosing to get dressed.

style statement

I choose style, every day.

owning your confidence

STRIPPING DOWN

I'll never forget the first time I went to an all-female Korean spa. You know, one where everyone is naked? Like *naked*, naked. My best friend was getting married in three days, and a trip to the spa before the wedding had been her bridal request. I wouldn't have missed it for the world, even if I was horrified at the idea of standing completely bare in front of other women.

My whole life I've always had a love-hate relationship with my body. I love my body. I hate my body. I love my body and back again. Even with that yo-yo of emotions, I don't think I ever thought I had a beautiful body. I was shorter than everyone else, rounder than everyone else; I didn't think I was very pretty. I had different kinds of lumps and bumps and scars and cellulite and a little chub around the middle. When I looked in the mirror that's all I could really focus on. What I saw were all my imperfections.

So here I am, days before my best friend's wedding, the most exciting day of her life *and mine* because, my goodness, we've known each other since we were twelve years old! And in an act of love for her, I decided to defy my fears, walk into a Korean spa, and stand completely naked for everyone to see. I am terrified.

At the spa lockers they give you an itty-bitty towel, and that is it. All the women in the locker room are whimsically stripping off their clothes in anticipation of body freedom. Oh, to be free of the confines of wardrobe! Frankly, I like being in my clothes! I hesitantly peel each item off me, one by one, trying to hide my skin as it's revealed with my tiny towel—to no avail! The towel doesn't cover anything. Not to mention I'm totally overdue for a bikini wax. *Great.* I have taken so long to get undressed that now I have to walk into the spa room in all my nakedness *all alone.*

I stand at the top of the room with my arms clinched to my sides and my hands covering my lady bits. Taking itty-bitty steps, I slowly shuffle my feet, with my back slightly arched, using my arms and hands to hide whatever I can. Wow. This is a big moment. From the outside looking in, I'm fit for an Amy Schumer–style comedy sketch.

Then I see my best friend's loving, accepting, and smiling face peering out of a steamy spa, along with her sister and a few close friends from childhood. She lights up when I walk in, and says, "Just come on in, Laurie! It feels amazing!" She knows how nervous I am to be so exposed.

I quickly toss my towel to the side and make a mad dash into the tea-tinted water of the Jacuzzi. All I can think about when I walk down the staircase is *if I hold on to the rail, then I can't hide behind my hands anymore!* What if people see my rolls when I bend to walk down the stairs without slipping? What if people notice that my breasts are slightly two different sizes? What if people see how ugly my body is?

As I submerge up to my shoulders in the warm embrace of the jacuzzi, my bestie says, "See, that wasn't so bad, was it?"

Um, yeah. Yeah it was.

So there I sit, chatting with the girls, feeling so happy to be under the water and protected by the blurry view caused by the bubbles and waves. As I lie back in the water, I survey the room—there are SO many naked women! I honestly don't think I have ever been in a situation like this before. Plus, every woman is so different. I see straight waists and curvy derrieres. I see C-section and breast augmentation scars. Small breasts and big breasts. Balanced shapes and unbalanced shapes. I see cellulite and rolls. I see mature skin and youthful skin. I see size 0 *and* size 24. But there is something they all have in common. They all effortlessly walk in and out of the hot tubs, saunas, steam rooms, and showers without even flinching, their heads held high, a strut in their step, and a quiet confidence in their vibe. I'm so taken aback by all the individual body love and acceptance in this room. Beautiful women with beautiful bodies of all shapes and sizes! And here I am, cowering in the corner, dreading the moment one of the girls says, "Hey! Let's switch to one of the sauna rooms."

As I continue to observe all the women around me, I begin to feel inspired. These women are truly embracing who they are and the bodies they are in. Everybody and every *body* is so different. Yet all the women are standing proudly, owning who they are, and in total love with and acceptance of the body they have.

It hits me: If they are okay with their bodies of all different shapes and sizes, then what's wrong with my body and its shape and size? *Nothing!* We are all beautiful! As I pop in and out of the different hot tubs and spa rooms, I find myself standing a little more confidently with each step. This whole experience is like a giant blinking neon sign to myself: *Love your body for what it is. Love yourself for who you are!*

I remember leaving that day in a completely different mood. When I walked out, I wasn't using my arms to hide my body anymore. Instead, I was standing tall with my arms at my hips, in Wonder Woman pose. I felt invincible. I felt beautiful, I felt confident, and I felt fearless. My body was beautiful just the way it was; I am beautiful just the way I am. And it took this very, *very* naked experience for me to see the light of the confidence already shining within me.

CULTIVATING CONFIDENCE

So, do you still think this is just a book about style? Actually, it's about cultivating confidence, wearing your confidence, and totally owning it from the inside out, all disguised in a style survival manual. Yes, that's right. *Shhhh. Don't tell anyone. Actually, tell everyone!* The more confident women there are taking the streets, the more positive change we can create for us all. But let's dial this back and start by looking at confidence with a fresh, open mind. So, what is confidence?

Confidence is an unadulterated self-awareness, an ownership and belief in yourself. It's what you stand for and how you express that message. It is the acceptance of who you are, what you look like, and where you are in your life no matter what it took to get there. Confidence is the inner glow you feel when you are in total alignment with your best you. It's that bright, energetic light that shines through your wardrobe and out into the world. It is knowing you are whole and owning every little ounce of you fully—all the choices you've made, all the decisions you will make, the woman you used to be, the woman you are today, the body you have, how your body will change over time, and especially the woman you continue to grow and evolve to be. It is taking possession of yourself and your life, no matter what your story is, and letting your true, brightest self shine through.

Confidence is a key component of style, and style is your tool to continue to cultivate, nurture, and support your confidence. *See how that works there?* Confidence and style work hand in hand. Without confidence, your style won't shine; without your own personal sense of your style, your confidence doesn't glow as bright. Confidence and style are the secret sauce, and together they create everyday magic, positivity, and possibilities in your life. Your conviction of who you are, what you are, and the story you tell will emanate your confidence. But building that confidence is really a very simple task that has a heavy weight to bear. It's super uncomfortable! As you've learned, you have to get uncomfortable and do it consistently to make yourself more comfortable doing it. Getting uncomfortable is all about action. First, you must identify the things that make you feel like your best *you*, from dressing your best you to owning yourself fully.

The hardest part is simply starting, then choosing to do it again the next day and the next day. I've learned that the hardest path in life will always have the greatest benefits. The easier path is easy for a reason, right? The more challenging path inevitably forces you to build resilience, durability, and strength, gifting you a feeling of accomplishment when you get through to the other side. That is why taking action is an influential tool to cultivating your confidence—which is why I wrote this book. It's essentially a roadmap to create and own your confidence!

Confidence comes from a feeling of certainty. How do you feel certain? By knowing what you *can* do and *how* you can do something. These tools are to help give you a sense of certainty. With that certainty, you shift into confidence. I want to teach you practical and easy tools you can put into action immediately. By the end of this book I want you to be certain that you are making the best style choices for yourself, ones that support your growth and brighten your life, all the while having the fun, motivational, and badass teacher to inspire you to do it over and over and over again. *Oh hey! That's me! You got this, girl!*

Don't feel confident right now? By working on *you*, you can feel more and more of the confidence that comes from within. Feeling confident is a practice, and it can be built up, even if you don't feel that way. Tomorrow, *I dare you* to put on an outfit that makes you feel fantastic. That one outfit you've been saving for a special meeting or event, go wear it for the day. No, really! Just step into a little bit of Stylepowerment and see how you feel. You can utilize the tools of style to pump up yourself, your mood, and your energy level, just by honoring who you are. It's that certainty of putting on the best look for you each day that will continue to empower you as you try new things, get creative, and evolve through your Stylepowerment journey!

BODY CONFIDENCE

The powerful essence of confidence comes from many pillars that all stand together to create the fullness of the energy. One of those pillars is body confidence, which is a really challenging topic for so many women. Let's dive in headfirst!

What if I told you that your body is beautiful?

Yes, *your* body. The body you have right now, at this moment. Not the body that is waiting for that last ten to fifteen pounds to be just right.

Not the body you had when you were twenty. Not the body you had the day you got married. Not the body you would like to have in the future after adding the planned diet and workout regimen to your schedule. Your body *today*. The body you have as you read this paragraph. THAT beautiful body. And if you are going to live out your best life with a confident style that reflects the most glowing version of you, then you are also going to have to embrace that beautiful body of yours, no matter what state it is in.

Creating body confidence always comes with a little resistance because our relationship with our body is such an intimate and vulnerable one. For all the "imperfections" we verbalize, the insecurities informed by outside sources, and the negative self-talk, we take those words to heart and they sting. In the private work I do with women, I consistently witness the most incredible, beautiful women looking in the mirror and not seeing what I see. Instead, they see their tired eyes, their hard-to-lose pounds, their maturing skin, their changing bodies, their scars, their hips, their legs, their arms, and everything they are insecure about in between. *Sound familiar?*

To observe women, and even myself at times, speaking in such self-deprecating ways reminds me how powerful words can be in our lives. Those words then resonate and, over time, become our truth and dictate our style choices and self-expression. Knowing this reminds me why it is so important to embrace our bodies first before we do anything to support our style. We must find the confidence within to see how beautiful we already are.

We all have something we don't love about our bodies. To put this in context, for the hundreds of women I have personally worked with one-on-one in my private styling practice, 100 percent of them had *something* they didn't love about their bodies. Whether they were a size 2 or a size 20, there was always something that came up about them. *And. That. Is. Okay!* It's entirely normal, it's very real, and it's ours.

Want to know something ironic? This section has been the hardest one for me to write. While I've had quite the journey learning how to own my own confidence in all areas of myself, that doesn't mean I don't still succumb to my personal insecurities from time to time. The devastating part is how feeling insecure about myself and my body makes me question my worth. So what do I do? I fight it off by wearing my most fabulous outfit with a colorful shoe, something that not only makes me feel like me but also reminds me that I *am me*. It's that action forward for myself that can make all the difference as I head out the door for my day, especially those mornings when I'm in tears over it all. Getting dressed empowers you. That's the Stylepowerment! This is how you take the control and continue to reframe your mind, your outlook on yourself, and your style.

Your body is BEA-U-TI-FUL. Your body is a living, breathing miracle. Think about all the functions your body performs that you don't even have to think about: blood circulation, digestion, skin renewal, the beating of your heart. That is incredible. And now after having a baby, I understand my body even more. My body created a human; I didn't do anything! I just ate, slept, cried (a lot) and my incredible body did all the work. We are all miracles moving around each and every day. And the miracle body you have, no matter what you may feel about it, is magic.

In working with women over the last ten years, this has become apparent to me: loving our bodies is an integral part of style, and our style is an integral part of our souls' expression to the world. This realization hits home every time I have an opportunity to work with and style a breast cancer survivor. These women are incredible. Each styling session with them has touched my soul more profoundly than any other appointment. These women have personally been through the most body-challenging experiences, from mastectomies, surgeries, and complications to chemotherapy, radiation, and recovery. It is an experience that is so intimate that it can cut deep into the soul of a woman, challenging her to see her value as a woman and her status as a woman. While these women have survived the odds, they still endure a genuine feeling of loss—they lost touch with the beautiful, powerful, and alluring women that they are.

Rosie, one of the survivors I've had the honor to work with, is beautiful inside and out. But when I met her, she didn't feel that way. When looking in the mirror, she could only see her scars, her physical loss from her mastectomy, and the extra weight her body took on during the process. Each day when she got dressed, she faced her body in the mirror with a feeling of loss for the woman she once was. Where women see loss, I see opportunity. Where women see pain, I see powerful transformation. In our style session together, I was able to show her a new way to look at herself and her body.

First, we needed to address the reality of Rosie's body. We talked about everything from the scars to the bra inserts to how she didn't feel like a woman anymore. We also talked about her body having endured the challenge of cancer and surviving. Her body carries her from point A to point B. Her body carried her two children. Her body is what makes her the woman she is now. Most importantly, her body is strong, powerful, female, and beautiful just the way it is. The woman in the mirror is a survivor and a warrior.

Many women are not fully educated on how to style for their body type and flatter the figure they currently have. I taught Rosie how to do just that. (Don't worry, you'll get to learn too!) Flattering the figure you currently have has the magic to show you your frame in a whole new light. You can see that what you thought were flaws to your frame can be styled to flatter your figure. And each individual is different. For Rosie, she specifically needed waist definition, an acceptance of her curvy body, and the right kind of silhouettes to frame it. We put all that together in her look.

Another challenge Rosie had was that she had a scar near her underarm that made her feel uncomfortable, so she refused to wear anything sleeveless. By teaching her how to layer and how to spot the kind of tops that would work for her, new opportunities opened up for her that she hadn't tried before. The overall process was about showing Rosie that she was still the beautiful woman she had always been.

Regardless of Rosie's perceived body challenges, there was a way to work with it so that she could style herself to feel confident. I showed her how to layer, how to define her waist, how to elongate her frame, and how to strategically draw attention to the areas she loved about her body. As much time as we spent together discussing her challenges, we also spent time talking about what she loved about her body—specifically, her smile.

Of course, I had to say, "What if your wardrobe made you smile more?"

She looked at me with eyes of hope.

"Girl, it's possible!"

We styled outfit after outfit together. There was magic even in the simplest of outfits. When Rosie saw herself wearing a dress, jacket, and belt combination that flattered her figure and covered up her scar, she felt like a woman again. It was a priceless moment. Never did she imagine that she could wear anything like this before. And it didn't just make her feel good—it made her glow. Her smile is now a permanent part of her outfits.

The transformative power of style is a game-changer, but to transform, we have to

love our bodies for every little everything. Imperfections and all! Can you stand in the mirror naked and face yourself? Can you say "I love you" to your body and truly mean it? Once you begin to love every aspect of your body and embrace your body confidence, that is when we can begin the educational journey to style your body in a way that flatters your unique figure. On the other side of this body breakthrough, there is magic, and it's all yours for the taking!

THE STYLE WITHIN

This topic is literally why I continue to do what I do as a personal stylist. I started LaurieBstyle knowing that style can build confidence. It has proven time and time again to be the most potent magic potion for creating possibilities in our lives. Owning your confidence is not something to fear but instead something to cultivate, grow, and continue to build for yourself. Because it's right there waiting for you—a door to unlock! But I also think finding your confidence builds your style equally. Like I said in the very beginning of the chapter, style and confidence go hand in hand. You can't have one without the other. When you wear an outfit with style, you can spark that confidence, and when you feel that glowing confidence from within, girl, you've got style!

I always say, "If you believe, then I will believe." Meaning if you truly believe down to your bones in who you are, how you are expressing yourself, and what you are doing in this world, then you can make anyone believe in anything you want them to know. When you are whole with who you are, what you put on your body to express your best *you*, it can make anyone catch the vibe you are sending! It doesn't matter whether your style is upscale casual, sophisticated professional, bohemian badass, vintage-inspired eclectic, or athleisure chic—or all of those things! If you are rocking your style, you can't help but burst and beam with confidence.

It's that kind of high-vibrational and positive personal energy that reverberates not just around you but in your day-to-day life. Oh hey, the Law of Attraction! That is why your style from within has such an impact. It's not about looking fashionable or even dressing to the nines. It's about you, getting to dress your best you, feeling fantastic while you do it, strutting your confidence as you head out the door, and putting that powerful energy out into the world. Imagine the possibilities.

so, let's recap!

- We come in all shapes and sizes. Nothing like getting naked at a spa to truly experience that notion.

- Confidence is self-awareness, ownership, and belief in yourself. It's what you stand for, how you self-express, and the acceptance of where you are in your life no matter what it took to get there.

- Body confidence is a vital part to our personal confidence perspective. But our perception of ourselves can mask our reality and break down our confidence and view of self-worth. Just remember this: You are a walking miracle, girl! That's incredible!

- Confidence and style are a secret sauce. Together they work in a symbiotic relationship not only to show off your best you but also to let that essence exude from within. Style is your outer representation of your inner self. When your confidence glows through you radiate positivity. And when you radiate positivity, positivity will find you.

style statement

I radiate my beauty, confidence, energy, and uniqueness through wardrobe and self-expression. On days I need a confidence boost, I use wardrobe to help me shine.

PART II

face yourself, then love yourself

confronting your closet

CLOSET RELATIONSHIP STATUS:
"IT'S COMPLICATED"

Your style tells your story, and we all have one to share—the story of the absolutely amazing you! But the clothes in our closets don't always tell that story. Instead, they are clothes that carry stories of their own, and as you face your closet each and every morning, those stories can have an entirely different agenda altogether: to weigh you down and dim your light.

What's your relationship status with your closet? Many will say, "It's complicated!" Know the feeling? Oh, we've all been there. Let's say the infamous phrase together now: I HAVE NOTHING TO WEAR!!! Those painful, frustrating, running-late-again, overwhelmed, and sometimes manic fits over this horrible five-word sentence are a collective experience we all share. The feeling creeps up slowly as you start to review the contents of your closet.

It begins to heat up as you put a few things on that don't look or feel right. Then the panic and sweat roll in as you continue to try option after option to no avail. Standing in front of your closet paralyzed and *naked,* you then run frantically over to your dresser. *Maybe there is something in here that will work.* You pull out your folded denim, T-shirts, tank tops, and knit items, but instead of building an outfit, you build a mountain of clothing on the floor and feel more lost! So you head back to stand in front of your closet again, staring blankly at the clothes hanging in front of you. Stuck. Motionless. Ready to cry. *Fun times!* With a closet full of clothes, and the feeling of utter frustration as your style guide, it is no wonder we just throw our hands up and stop with the effort altogether.

I wish I could share with you one specific moment when I was faced with my closet and had some big epiphany that changed my life, but there wasn't one standout moment, because this experience haunts me over and over again. I remember as early as elementary school when I was hysterically crying, running late to school, completely undressed, and not even close to heading out the door with my mom. She would call from the other room, "Get dressed, Laurie! You're going to be late!"

Well, I'm happy to report, much to the chagrin of my sweet mom, and now my husband, that nothing has changed! Yep! I sometimes still let my closet get the best of me, and it affects not only what I wear for the day but also how I *feel*. While this may be a shocking closet confession coming from an experienced stylist, I wouldn't have it any other way. It's what makes me so good at what I do, because *I get it.* I've been there. I've whined, I've complained, I've pulled everything out of my closet and thrown it to the floor. I've stood naked in frustration and jumped back under my sheets in tears. I've ugly cried at the end of my bed in my bra and underwear. I've gotten a fresh face of makeup and mascara smeared all over my pillowcase. I've thrown my clothes across the room. I've left piles of outfits that didn't work all over the floor and on my husband's side of the bed (sorry, honey!). I've tried on ten outfits only to go back to the original outfit that I tried on.

I've given up and just worn all black. I've changed an entire outfit because I could not find the right purse to go with it. I've stayed home feeling foolish because my clothes and closet got the best of me.

All this anguish has opened my eyes to the deeper challenge we all face when we open our closet doors. It's not just "I have nothing to wear." It's a mind game we play with ourselves that puts us into this state of wardrobe worry. Here's the reality check: all of this chaos has nothing to do with the actual clothes in your closet. The frustration instead comes from the *feelings* that arise when we see our clothes.

Remember all those rules in your head, clogging up your mind? They go deeper than just a passing list of a few rules and regulations you can run through. Our closets are like deep, cavernous black holes of insecurities, memories, feelings, and constant reminders of all kinds of things, good and bad. Each morning when you get dressed, you are not only confronting your closet, you are confronting yourself.

Each item in your closet tells a story about you and your life. A story about when you bought it, why you bought it, why you wear it all the time, why you never wear it, when you wore it last, how many times you've worn it, or that one time you finally put it on! Crazy, right? Whether you are aware of it or not, your subconscious becomes a stuffed file cabinet of thoughts, and each clothing item you look at can open a fresh drawer of feelings, introspection, and judgment.

No wonder we get closet paralysis! **When we judge our clothes, we are judging ourselves.** Let's take a walk through the closet, shall we? Let's pull open those doors and take a look inside. What do you see? Is it that sequined top you spent a lot of money on but still haven't worn yet? You just HAD to have it, but when you see it you feel guilty for spending so much money on that one item and still don't know when you're going to wear it. The tags are still on!

Then there is the infamous pair of ride-or-die jeans that don't fit anymore. You wore them all the time, on dates, to events, on Saturday strolls and evenings out with the ladies . . . months ago. And there they hang, right in front of you. Every time you pass them when choosing what to wear in the morning you say to yourself, *Ugh, I feel so fat right now.* You put the jeans on, just in case something has changed. Nope! It's gotten worse! A lovely reminder of your ever-changing body.

What about that dress from your early twenties you are still holding on to? You haven't worn that dress in years. There it sits, taunting you every morning and reminding you of the glory days. Or what about that frilly ruffled blouse you wore on that terrible, horrific, no-good date? The one where you knocked a glass of wine over, coughed out a piece of shrimp cocktail across the table, felt like you were pulling teeth to have a conversation, and then he asked for you to split the dinner bill? *Ugh!* I *hate* that! Another reminder of a negative situation that sits with you on the daily. Those ruffles will always make you think of that night. *Wonderful.*

What about those outrageous colored pants you just couldn't leave the store without? When you purchased them, they were *juuuuust* a little small. So you said to yourself, *I'll buy them now, and when I lose those last few pounds, I'll be able to wear them! Yay!* Except they still don't fit. They hang in your closet as a reminder that you still have a way to go on your health journey and that you shouldn't have been so impulsive in the first place.

I could go on! But we all have something that triggers us when we open up the closet doors. What you have to wear isn't good enough, your body isn't slim enough, or you are not *enough.* From that morning mindset mess, you inform yourself of what to wear for the day. It's no wonder the simple act of getting dressed has become a challenge for so many women.

THE MORNING EXPERIENCE

Are you ready for a life-changing realization? Your outfit isn't the only thing accompanying you on your way out into the world; your morning mood follows you too. Those complex, sometimes indescribable feelings that are conjured up by opening your closet doors are like loud, clanking, oversized accessories: you didn't want to wear them, but you're stuck wearing them all day anyway. They are nagging, controlling, and often dictating what you should wear for the day, then sticking around for the ride! From work, to meetings, to appointments, to networking, to events, to dinners and dates! When you have a negative experience with yourself and your closet in the morning, that stays with you throughout the day. Simply put, your morning experience determines your day.

But you are so comfortable with the routine you know, and the idea of empowering your style to make you feel good seems like a nonexistent reality, so you gravitate to the clothes that support your current mindset, and you stay stuck in the pattern. This experience is so habitual you don't even realize it is happening! Day after day you pull out the same items from your wardrobe to wear because at this point you *literally can't even*. We all live in the statistic. We wear 20 percent of our closet 80 percent of the time. Yeah, let that one sink in.

So here's the thing: you *have* to get dressed in the morning. You absolutely, unequivocally HAVE to get dressed in the morning. You have to. Every morning! By societal standards, yes, you have to cover your body before you leave the house. Well, technically, you *could* leave the house naked, shock your neighbors, become the talk of the town, and then have the cops show up and arrest you for indecency. *Oh hey, Officer!* Now, if that scenario doesn't sound good to you, then we are back to square one. You have to confront your closet and get dressed every morning. You must decide what you are going to wear for the day. Yep, whether you like it or not, you have to get dressed.

Let's take this another step further. What happens when you get to work after a routinely uninspired morning or continue on your errands or duties for the day? How do you feel? Do you feel like a wallflower? Unfeminine? Do you feel envious of other people and how "put together" they look? Do you feel insecure? Do you feel mediocre? Most importantly, how do you *want* to feel?

These thoughts and feelings come up for all of us from time to time, or let's be honest, all of the time, and that is some hefty baggage to carry around with you every day. Physically, we show signs of it in how we stand, how we carry ourselves, and how we present ourselves. Energetically, we show how we feel about ourselves and how we approach ourselves. These nonverbal cues are what other people can sense about you based on your overall appearance. It's not just the clothes that reveal your insecurity story; it's your energy and essence too.

Understanding this is one of the biggest mindset shifts that can take place for you. Because when you realize that getting dressed is affecting your day, then I bet you will want to take steps to change that day destiny you felt trapped in. And I'm here to tell you that you are NOT trapped. You are in total control, and I am here to support you through it! You are going to step-by-step take back control of your closet, your closeted emotions, and your personal style; and you are going to OWN yourself, your confidence, and your life as you live the life of your dreams and set an example for other women.

CLOSET CONFESSIONAL

Our closets are our most intimate spaces. This is something I'm super sensitive to when I'm cleaning out closets, because this is where things get very personal. I learn everything about my clients inside their closets. Their closets always reveal to me not just their style challenges through their stories but also some of their deepest-rooted insecurities that are holding them back from living their fullest lives. Cleaning out these dark corners is the first step to creating a powerful light that illuminates the pathway to your potential! Unlocking that potential in your wardrobe, reconnecting you to who you truly are, and revealing the powerful possibilities in your life are what I live for.

There is a reason why my personal philosophy is "People first, style second." I give such heart and care to this initial part of the styling process. Understanding, acknowledging, and cleaning out your closet will set you up for true style success. This isn't about the clothing or the style; it is about the feelings we hold, misperceptions we claim to be real, and the unsupportive stories we tell ourselves, stopping ourselves before we can even get going. And women deserve better. You deserve to break through!

One instance in particular comes to mind: My client Taryn had a closet full of clothes and stories to boot. Up until we had our appointment, Taryn was in a serious rut. She didn't feel good, she didn't feel like herself, and every day she was making choices for her style that didn't make her happy. Her overall demeanor was timid, shy, and a little frightened. As we went through her closet, Taryn would share an individual story for each piece, as if she had to justify her closet to me. She shared what the piece meant to her, why she had kept it so long, and on and on. Between the lines, I could hear that she felt deeply insecure about herself and her wardrobe. Every time she left the house for the day, she carried that insecurity and heavy doubt with her.

As we continued our private work together, Taryn opened up and finally revealed that she had been brought up with a verbally abusive family member. Since her childhood, this family member had always put her down, continuing now into her thirties. After all these years, she never felt worthy, nor did her wardrobe. Her closet became a dark vacuum of pain. She hadn't ever seen herself as the beautiful woman that she was. Instead, she believed what was told to her: that she was overweight, unattractive, and worthless. With these painful words and memories, Taryn felt that what she wore always reflected how she felt.

While deep in her closet, I pulled out a multitiered hanger with four dresses on it. The dresses were dark in color, messy in pattern, and shapeless.

I asked Taryn, "What's the story with these dresses?"

She replied, "Oh, those are my ugly dresses."

"Ugly dresses?!" I said in shock.

"Yes, whenever I am feeling ugly, I wear those dresses."

"How does wearing these dresses make you feel before you step out the door?"

She took a deep breath and sighed. "Terrible."

I kept poking. I mean, that is why I do what I do—to help people break through! "Then why do you wear them?"

"Because when I am feeling ugly, they are ugly too, and then they match my mood."

It was heartbreaking to hear. She didn't deserve that. She deserved better. She deserved to feel beautiful, strong, and confident. So we did the strongest thing together, even though it took a little convincing! I had Taryn throw the four dresses one by one into the donation bag. *Goodbye and good riddance!* Never again would Taryn use clothes to support her insecurities, not if I had anything to do with it.

Once we were done with the clean-out phase, we took a look through what we'd kept and discussed why. In the depths of her closet, I uncovered two pencil skirts. They were fitted and high waisted, one in black and one in magenta. I thought, *Bingo! Now we've got something here.* Taryn shared with me that she never wore them. She bought them because she wanted to wear them out while dating but hadn't had the confidence to do so. She would wear jeans and a knit top untucked to hide her frame instead. I told her to put one of the skirts on, and I handed her a striped knit top left from her closet purge. She zipped up the skirt, layered the shirt over the skirt, turned to me, and shrugged her shoulders. I instructed her to tuck her shirt into the skirt; then I pulled out a belt to sit at her high waist. As I buckled the last notch of the belt, I turned Taryn to the mirror. Her eyes lit up!

She looked at me and said, "Is *this* me?" Cue the waterworks!

"Yes, it is! Look at how beautiful you are! Look at your female form! Look at your smile!" I paused and let her take it in. Then I said, "Now imagine that you can look and feel like this *every day.*"

"You mean, I can do that?" Her face was lighting up.

"Of course you can! You can do and be anything with your style, especially if it makes you glow."

In our session together, we built outfit after outfit, look after look, playing with her skirts, jeans, tops, cardigans, belts, colorful flats, and fun necklaces. Everything from wearing tonal colors together to mixing prints with her floral blouses and leopard shoes to wearing a colored belt with every outfit. In just a half day, Taryn went from being a wallflower to blossoming beyond her wildest dreams. She had always wanted to look and feel feminine, sexy, and beautiful. All those things were already inside her. It just took some self-reflection, leaving her comfort zone, learning new techniques, and having an open mind to get her to break through to her most vibrant self.

Her self-love and self-care journey continued to grow and blossom as she began to feel like her true self: energetic, captivating, and happy. A month later, Taryn was happy to report that when she had seen her abusive relative at a family gathering, the person had complimented her on how lovely she looked. A first ever and a beautiful new beginning for a woman who deserves to experience the world with self-love, beauty, and possibility.

RECONNECTING WITH YOUR CLOSET

It's officially time you take back your control, reconnect to your closet, and ultimately reconnect with yourself. We are easily influenced by emotional triggers, and that gets in the way of our morning experience. One of the hardest parts about cleaning out our closets is just the idea of "letting go." And just like you got full permission from me to throw out all the fashion rules bogging you down, you also get full permission to LET GO of the clothes that are holding you back. You do not have to hold on to anything you don't love anymore. You don't have to keep anything that brings up negative emotions, stories, or thoughts. You do not have to wear anything that doesn't make you feel like the most amazing you. It's time to free yourself from this tether. Imagine what you can create when you are free from a wardrobe that brings you down.

Are you ready to face your own closet? We all have those dark corners with a blouse balled up in it that we haven't seen in years and didn't even realize was hiding back there. Well, we are going to pull her out and let her have her day in the sun. It is so important to see what we can dig up, clean out, and throw out because, by facing your closet, you get the opportunity to clear out the old the wardrobe *and* the negative energy buildup that has collected over the years.

First and foremost, we must look at our wardrobes with a nonjudgmental eye. Taking a more analytical approach helps cut out the emotion a bit and helps cut to the chase. Here's something to remember: It doesn't matter whether you bought it off-price or you paid a fortune, or if it is the most sparkly item in your closet or the gorgeous dress you wore a few years back. **If it doesn't flatter your frame, fit you well, and meet your personal style vibe, then it's time to let it go.** But if it fits beautifully, leads to a smile, and causes you to do a double take at yourself in the mirror, *then* it's a keeper. I only want you to wear clothing that makes you feel happy and be the confident woman you've always wanted to portray.

If the thought of cleaning out your closet is already giving you sweaty palms and heart palpitations, don't worry, girl! I got you! There are so many different ways to clean out a closet, but I want to make it clear and simple.

First, make it a date! Schedule your closet cleanout time in your calendar. This is YOU time! You can even invite a trusted friend to join you. Having a subjective pair of eyes can help support you to make more confident decisions about your style. Play some great music, have a glass of wine or something bubbly (even infused sparkling water), and remember to be honest but have fun. You are not just cleaning out your closet, you're clearing out the old to make way for the new, abundant you!

Next, it's time to dive deep! Let's start with a very important first question to ask as you go through each item in your wardrobe one by one.

Do you love it? Emotional and straightforward. Do you love it? Yes or no. Ever hear the saying "If it's not a 'hell yes!' then it's a 'hell no'? That applies here perfectly. Trust your gut and you'll never go wrong. Very simply put: If you don't love it, why are you holding on to it? Dive into that question, and you may find that you are holding on to it for the wrong reasons. Especially if you start to answer no to the following questions.

Does it fit? This is a fundamental and technical question. If you don't know how to answer this based on your current body type, there is a whole chapter on fit I wrote just for you. Chapter 6 will break it all down for you. But in the meantime, here are some things to think about for each item without getting into the nitty-gritty of the topic. When you put the item on, does it go on with ease? Is the zipper a breeze? Does it flow with your frame? Does it feel comfortable *and* empowering? Does it accentuate your waist and flatter your beautiful figure? If you answer no to these questions, then these are definitely pieces ripe for the goodbye pile. Cue music. Cue Elsa. "Let it go! Let it go!" Yeah, I couldn't resist.

Here's another way to think about the fit of your garments as you continue to clean out. Does it feel like a chore to pull it over your head and chest? Or does zipping the pants cause the dreaded muffin top, pull at the fabric, or even cause the pants to ride up in the middle. *Oh, you know what I'm talking about.* Also take a good look; while the item may "fit" and be comfortable, does it actually hide and/or distract from your body? Basically, when you put it on, does it make you look and *feel* larger than you are?

Ready for more things to think about?

Is it in good condition? This one is a big culprit in our closets as we tend to hold on to things for a very long time. So if it's worn, torn, tired, dated, faded, sloppy, or ill-fitting, or if the fabric has pills, holes, or stains—goodbye! Yes, it's that simple. You can't un-fade a black, or un-pill an old knit top when it's been through the wringer. Here's what I like to say when I get to those items in any closet. While you may be saying goodbye to them, remember that they have been worn with lots and lots of love, which is why they are so worn! And when they have been worn with so much love, they get tired and it's time for them to retire. Here's another twist on the topic to think about (I wasn't kidding when I said we were going to have to go deep): When you wear clothes that are tired, dated, worn, et cetera, they actually devalue the overall look you are presenting. Wearing them in your everyday wardrobe doesn't serve to help you step into your best you; instead, they are holding you back from shining! When you think about those items like this, the process of saying goodbye feels a lot easier, and it's empowering! Goodbye, dowdy, sad, faded, and dated. Hell-o, glowing new me!

Is it still relevant (meaning age, work, and lifestyle appropriate)? This is a loaded question as your opinion may come into play, swaying your decision, which is why it may be helpful to have a friend or even a stylist, like myself, there to give you an outside view as you assess your clothes.

Here is what I want you to consider when it comes to your clothes: Does the item fit your lifestyle? Are you wearing it for work? For fun? Are you wearing it at all? Does the item fit your style sensibility in your current circumstances? Is it age appropriate for you?

Does it feel like the YOU, you are today? We all evolve over time, and so do our style choices. What you loved to wear and what used to fit your vibe a few years back may not be where you are now, either in your day-to-day life or even professionally. Also consider where you WANT your life to be. Does the item fit that future vision for yourself? If you can't answer yes to these questions, then the item isn't serving you and thus is perfect for the goodbye pile.

And lastly, this final question is the big emotional question you are allowed to ask, and I believe, above all else, it should be considered for everything you put on your body:

When you put it on, can you say, "I FEEL LIKE ME"? You have to *feel* like you are your absolute best, most shining *you* in the clothes you wear. I mean, why should you wear anything less? It's simple but super important.

Ready for a new layer to support you in the process? As you go through and answer your questions, you will be simultaneously organizing five piles. I call this the "Five-Pile Method."

1) **Your keepers.** These are the items you love. They fit, they flatter, they support your current lifestyle and style sensibilities, they are in great condition, and, most importantly, they make you feel confident, fabulous, and like your best you!

2) **Your seasonals.** These fit all the criteria of a keep, but they aren't currently in your everyday rotation of style. For example, occasion

dresses, seasonal items, heavy coats, holiday gear, vacation pieces, work items you may need down the line—all assuming that they check off the correct criteria when cleaning out.

3) **Your menders.** Those items you love that are still relevant, still in great condition, and mostly still fit but need a small tailoring tweak here, a hem fix there, or a slimming line created all around.

4) **Your sentimentals.** These are those items that you are holding on to because they are meaningful in some way. You may never wear them again, but holding on to them gives you a beloved memory, a family history story, or an heirloom you want to share with your own children.

5) **Your goodbye pile.** Yes, it's time to say goodbye. They don't fit, they don't flatter, they are worn, tired, and out of date. Most importantly, they don't make you feel good when you wear them. Here is your permission to let go and say buh-bye. And if it helps, think about this: the clothing industry is the second-most wasteful industry in the world. By letting go of the clothes you don't wear anymore and donating them to an organization that can help people less fortunate, you are helping by reducing waste in the trash as well as the waste of more production needed to supply more clothing to everyone. So say goodbye with good vibes!

I'm not going to sugarcoat this: The closet cleanout can feel overwhelming. The whole process can bring up memories, insecurities, negative stories, and even sad feelings. But just think: as you clean those pieces out, you are taking away their power. And by identifying what they are, you are slowly but surely reconnecting to your closet and yourself in the process. Cleaning out your closet is the first big step in learning how to shine from the inside out. Because when you have removed these negative notions, and you wear clothes that make you feel great, you begin to shine from the inside out.

Wait, but now what? Don't worry, girl! I've got you! Here's what you are doing to do with your five piles.

The keeps: Hang them back in your closet front and center! Pop ahead to the next chapter to learn how to be organized! (Don't worry, I wouldn't leave you hanging there either!)

The seasonals: Depending on your closet situation, you can do a number of things. Organize them separately into a far back corner of your closet. Store them in a second closet. Fold up everything gently and put them into clear storage bins to store in your home where you have the appropriate space. (Those under-bed ones are lifesavers!) Or try the vacuum-pack space-saver bags if you are living in tight quarters! Basically, a quick solution for multiple situations.

The menders: Take them to the tailor, or sew small holes up on your own. Easy-peasy!

The sentimentals: These are ones to store away in a special drawer. Don't forget the lavender sashays and the cedar moth blocks!

The goodbye pile: There are a lot of ways to let go of your goodbye pile. But the most important thing you can do for yourself is to let it go! But seriously, you have no idea how many times I have heard from my clients that after we had a therapeutic closet cleanout session, they dipped right back into their goodbye pile for that feeling of familiar amid the day-to-day newness. Eventually, at the end of my appointments, I began to walk out of the house with all the bags of clothes to donate on my client's behalf. Because I knew! Oh, and they knew too!

Do your "today self" and your "future self" a favor by bravely saying goodbye. Look, it is not easy, but trust me, it is worth it! Don't forget to say goodbye with good vibes! Manifest the new you as you donate your clothes, allowing somebody less fortunate to find pieces that may fit her best self. You can even add icing on the empowerment cake by donating your best gently used clothes to organizations that support women in the workforce. That way, you know your donations will specifically support another woman reaching for her dream as well.

Reconnecting to your closet by cleaning out what doesn't serve you anymore also means you are acknowledging what you LOVE and bringing not just the fabulous clothes but the fabulous *you* to the forefront. Reconnecting to your closet actually is reconnecting with yourself! Your clothes should make you feel age appropriate, sophisticated, cool, interesting, feminine, flirty, sexy, powerful, whimsical, daring, exciting, and whatever your inner goddess desires (no matter your size)! I'd like you to sit with this idea: What would your life be like if you only wore clothes that made you feel all that powerful energy, all the time?

If you haven't figured it out yet, this process is totally a therapeutic exercise. You can think of it as cleansing all of those little negative nags that live inside your closet and your mind. They are not needed anymore, and it's up to you to bid them adieu. The chore may be daunting and painful, but by cleaning out each individual piece, you are letting go of the insecurities, bad memories, embarrassing experiences, and negative thoughts attached to them. Think about all the room you are making for new confidence, new energy, and new experiences to come into your life. Yes! By cleaning out your closet you are creating new possibility.

so, let's recap!

- Your wardrobe isn't just overflowing with clothes that don't serve you; it is holding old, stagnant energy too. Our closets are like those awful clingy fabrics that pick up threads, hairs, and lint wherever you go. But instead of lint, your closet is clinging to some of our deepest insecurities, memories, and feelings! Facing that every morning can affect your whole day ahead.

- The morning experience you have with yourself and your wardrobe is directly connected to your style choices, your mood, and the energy you give off for the day, and it's time we shift that energy into something empowering.

- Break down to break through, girl! No longer do you need to wear clothes that drain you or drag you down. Instead, you are allowed to wear clothes that make you feel fantastic, empowered, and like your best self.

- Reconnecting to your closet is a vital part of your Stylepowerment process. Even the simple, though deeply reflective, act of cleaning out your closet is the liberation you need from what holds you back. This will allow you to reconnect to what excites you and what energizes you.

style statement

I let go to grow by creating space in my closet for a new style and wardrobe that reflects my best me.

self-love — an act of style

THE SELF-CARE CHOICE

Let's talk about those special moments you take time to honor yourself, create space in your life, and treat yourself. *Oh, wait, you don't do that?* After this chapter you will. Because to me, self-care is directly related to our style. And get this: style is an act of self-care. What about the choice to take the time to get dressed? Yep, that is an act of self-care! Hey, reading this book is an act of style AND self-care! You are already on your way.

Like style, self-care is a choice. It's your choice to make a few extra minutes in the morning to do a dry brush or a body scrub in the shower. It's your choice to make space for a workout in the morning or at night. It's your choice to draw an evening bath with a glass of wine and a good book. It's your choice to schedule time away from your family to take care of yourself, even if it's just for thirty minutes to an hour. It's your choice to set money aside each month strictly for self-care services, like manicures and pedicures, massages, facials, foot rubs, a girls' spa day, or whatever else comes to mind. It's your choice to do this for you.

However, this is *waaaaay* easier said than done. How do I know? Because I am so guilty of it too! Adding acts of self-care into your life shouldn't be overwhelming, but I get why it feels that way. Who has EXTRA TIME? If you had extra time, you'd be doing all the things you never get to do, right? I get it! But the reality is, there is time. The point of self-care is to prioritize time for *you*. It's up to you to make the space for it, choose yourself first, and act on it.

Aaaaaah—the sound of "me time." That precious time you put aside just for yourself: to treat yourself to love on your body and to acknowledge the hard work you've put in. A few minutes here, a half hour there . . . Sounds blissful! There really is something so powerful about connecting to your core in order to support your best life. I get the struggle; it's uncomfortable to change your current patterns, but it is sometimes even more uncomfortable to put yourself first. And, girl, do I know this firsthand!

That said, let's start with something easy and not overwhelming to get you going. Think about it as small, simple steps that can make a huge impact over time. Do you think you can set aside one hour during the weekdays and two to three hours on the weekend just for you? It could be for anything, like getting a manicure and pedicure before you head home from work, or spending time in your closet to play dress-up and make a few outfits for the week ahead. Maybe you can wake up an hour early so that you can have your coffee or tea in the quiet and fresh air of the morning. Or it could even be to take a few extra minutes to put all your bathroom counter clutter away. Lord knows it's hard to get your face together in the morning when all your makeup, brushes, and Q-tips are strewn everywhere.

Just because we are talking about me time doesn't mean you have to do this alone. Your family or friends can be involved and support you in your self-care. Share your self-care plan with them! Not only will you have a support system to encourage you to take the time, but they can hold you accountable. Or if you have a partner and/or family at home, allow them to be a part of this self-care time for you by stepping in to take care of the home while you get a little time on your own. This openness about your needs can foster stronger communication and partnership, creating a happier more supportive energy around the home.

Quick reminder: *You deserve it!* You deserve all the me time you can create. It's really that simple. Creating *you* time on the daily and finding a self-care routine that feels good are big steps (disguised as small ones) toward your best life. By starting or ending your day with a loving activity that helps you feel a little better in this wild roller-coaster world we live in, you are upgrading yourself, your style, and your energy.

You deserve it!

YOU ARE THE STYLE!

LOVING THE SKIN YOU ARE IN

It is time we reacquaint ourselves with loving and appreciating the skin we are in. After all, this is what underlies our outfits each and every day. To truly love and honor your body is fundamental to the style you exude in your wardrobe. There are simple things you can do to help you get a little closer to that self-love and self-care that you not only need but totally deserve.

After my son was born my body, my style, and my whole life changed. (Oh hi, book number two!) I felt like I had lost myself entirely. A big part of that was how I felt in my body. Yes, my body created a miracle, but that didn't negate the deep-rooted insecurities coming to the forefront of my mind. And trust me, there is nothing more humbling in this process than living in granny panties. I mean, straight-up, ugly, high-waisted, full-coverage, visible-panty-line, 100 percent cotton granny panties. In a robe, they literally looked like they came past my waistline. My younger self never thought I'd live to see the day.

It took some time to learn to love my body again. Much of that time was spent embracing the granny-undergarment lifestyle. I mean, I had to—it was functional! And let's be honest: totally necessary. But it didn't make me feel good, and it definitely didn't make me *feel* like me. At some point, I finally broke. I had to get out of my comfortable granny panties and get uncomfortable again, literally and figuratively. I attribute the kick-start of my quest for self-love to my undergarment style shift. It wasn't until I finally invested in a few new bras and pairs of underwear that things started to change for me. I found bras that lifted the ladies and underwear that didn't cut into my soft sides, but instead lay gently on my skin, flowing with my frame and allowing me to see my body in a state of—dare I say?—sexiness.

And it hit me: What we wear underneath (whether you are working through that baby body or just a changing body) is a big part of how we view our own self-love. When we don't honor our body, when we don't embrace our body, we outfit our bodies in ways that don't serve our most loved selves. I'm not saying you need to embrace a black lace situation, but why not invest in matching undergarment sets that fit your frame best and make you feel sexy? Contrary to what some companies may make you think, your best undergarments shouldn't be worn for somebody else or just on a special occasion. Your underpinnings should be worn for YOU. For you to *feel* like you. For you to *see* you. For you to *be* you. Every day! Experiencing this can be a little spark to set you on the path toward more self-love. Your style survival depends on it!

When you don't give love to the skin you are in, you are dimming your own light. That's why, big or small, the absence of self-care matters as it can drain your power and drive. Anything from wearing clothes that don't make you feel good and eating poorly to not finding time to rest and pushing off exercise can drain you dry! But when you choose a healthier option—go to bed an hour early, read a book over watching TV, finally take that yoga class you've been wanting to try, treat yourself to a massage, or even get out of your comfort zone and finally try on a new size and style of undergarments to fit your current frame—that is when you feel an energy spark with a hint of motivation to do more. Feel-good acts are contagious. The more you do them the better and brighter you will feel.

Your acts of self-care will lead you straight to your self-love! This is why self-care is a key component to our style. Self-care fuels our self-love, and our self-love fuels our style.

Let's start by creating a stronger connection and getting back in touch with your body to give it the love and attention it deserves! Anything from rubbing your best lotion on your skin, to slathering on coconut oil right after a shower, to doing a body scrub once a week, to dry brushing your skin when you wake up. Being able to connect with your body on a sensory (and sensual) level is a literal act of self-love. Because with each hand stroke, or massage of your leg, or rub of your tummy, you are—perhaps unknowingly—acknowledging your body. The missing factor is the awareness that you have while doing it. Which, lucky for you, you can experience the next time you pull out the lotion!

Each time you put lotion on your skin, don't just quickly rub it in. Think about what you are doing. Acknowledge the body part you are giving extra love. Is it your feet? *Thank you, feet, for helping me stand all day and taking the steps to get me from one place to the next.* Is it your legs? Give them an extra massage and say to yourself, *Thank you so much, legs, for keeping me strong while carrying me throughout the day.* Is it your arms and hands? *Thank you! You carry my things, you write for me, you type and express for me during the workday . . .* You get the idea. By loving your body and acknowledging each part as you give it love and care, you are sending powerful signals to your brain to LOVE your body.

The more love you show your body, the more you will learn to love and appreciate your body. It's another muscle to flex and strengthen as you continue on your path. Do you have to be perfect at it? No. Do you have to militantly do this every day? No. Do you have to have it all figured out on day one? No. Instead, this is a *practice* that you can start at any time, continue to come back to when you need it, and exercise it as many times as you need it. Permission to be imperfect? *GRANTED.*

THE WHOLE LOOK

Your style is so much more than your clothing, your fashion, and closet. Style is all-encompassing. It's how you wear your clothes, how you feel about yourself in those clothes, and how you project your best you. But I would be remiss if I didn't touch upon a little bit of style and self-care fairy dust to sprinkle on top of every morning as you get dressed. In partnership with your wardrobe, a skincare, makeup, and hair routine not only elevates your overall outfit vibe but also supports your own empowerment. They, too, are acts of self-care. But if you are in the same boat as me, you've run into the problem of time, mood, effort, and lack of inspiration. Can't it all just be easy?! Truth is, it is easy, but it does require your attention and effort to make challenging tasks feel more seamless and routine over time. Cut out what is unnecessary and start with baby steps to build a foundation that feels good for you.

Let's start with your skin and makeup. It's time to explore a beauty regimen that allows you to honor your skin, eyes, and lips while opening up opportunities to see yourself in a fresh, new light. Personally, makeup has never been my forte. I would rather spend more time on my clothes than my face. However, when I neglect my skin and my face, I find I don't feel as great about my outfit overall. *It happens every time without fail!* I've also learned the hard way that when I don't do my makeup before I get dressed, it affects my perception of the outfit I created. When I am not taking care of my skin and face, it seems to directly affect my style. Yep. Entirely true.

So I taught myself a five-minute makeup routine. I researched skincare, concealer, and foundation that targeted what I wanted—like anti-aging, skin firming, and under-eye brightening—and I found a makeup palette that covers all the bases, from cheeks to highlighters to eyes and even a lip. One and done. Make it easy! It's so worth finding a skin-and-face routine that feels good for you. It's also important to invest in products that have as few chemicals as possible and will support your skin's vibrancy. But here's something I really love—getting educated! Sign up for a master class with your favorite makeup or skincare brand, or even hire a private makeup artist to come and teach you how to do an effortless, glowing face. That way, you will be well equipped as you make the total look a natural part of your routine.

The endless tutorials and educational videos online are a great option if you want to experiment in the privacy and comfort of your own home. Consider this a scheduled self-care me-time activity! Like the effort you will put into style, put even just a small dose of that effort into your gorgeous face too. The more you practice, the more you attempt that impossible cat eye, the more you play around with your blush and highlighter, the more you get creative with your multipurpose palettes, the easier it all becomes.

When it comes to your hair, it's the same thing. This is a scheduled self-care activity because hair especially can really make or break not just your outfit but also how you feel. Like makeup, easy hair styling can be taught. For me, I was always terrible at doing my hair. My best hair days used to be when I showered, toweled dry, and then headed out the door. I had the perfect natural wave. But over time my hair texture changed and those effortless beachy bohemian waves that magically appeared turned into a shapeless, frizzy mess—even when I have a good haircut! I became so fed up, I decided to ask my hairstylist, "Can you please just teach me how to curl my hair?" Step-by-step she showed me what to do. Then it was up to me to try it at home and then practice it again and again. Eventually, I mastered my locks.

Every hairstyle and hair texture is different, so there isn't one solution. And my personal hair experience by no means encapsulates the multitude of hair-styling needs of every girl. But asking for help if you need it is one of the first steps to getting the best support for you. Then invest in the tools or stylists that support a style that makes you shine.

What is most important is to allow yourself the space to try. Allow yourself acceptance in imperfection as you experiment to discover what works for you. Broken-record moment right here: the more you do it, the easier it becomes. I promise! I personally fought this extra effort for years, until I started to make the total look a part of my routine. Not because I needed to meet societal standards, but because I needed to for me—for how I saw myself in the mirror, for how I viewed myself as a woman, for how I perceived my overall style. There really is something to be said when you look in the mirror and don't like what you see. Unfortunately, it can be one small aspect that brings us down, and it takes the whole view of our beauty and shine down with it. By creating even just a little bit more space in your life to take care of yourself, however you can, you are cultivating that style from within that you can share with the world.

All of these small actions add up to something transformative. When you love the total look you've created, and you love what you see, that confident feeling shines through! As you see it more often, you begin to own it! Your time for self-care leads to more self-honor and self-love. The more honor and self-love you generate, the brighter you shine.

YOUR STYLE SANCTUARY

Getting excited to dive into your style survival manual? Just one more act of self-care that will support you in your style

success! Promise! This self-care activity is a getting-dressed game-changer. Ready? Time to design your personal style sanctuary. Think of this as an act of nesting into your next phase of Stylepowerment: the STYLE! We are diving back into your closet again because our work is not done in there. Let us make your closet feel bright and inspired and even be a place of zen. Remember your keepers pile? You are going to take that empowered and liberating closet cleanout one step further by organizing your clothes in a way that inspires you, excites you, and encourages you for more self-care *and* self-love.

You are going to make your closet your heart-happy place and no longer your dungeon of lost items, insecurity reminders, and negative thoughts. It should be a place of peace and creativity. When you open the doors you should feel joy, love, happiness, inspiration, and motivation to dress your best you.

But let's get real for a second. We both know that an organized closet can go from pristine to a train wreck in a matter of minutes. So don't forget to give yourself grace! Maintaining your sanctuary can feel like a chore at times, but if you look at it as another act of self-care, reconnection back to yourself, then you can shift your whole perspective and make each time with your closet meaningful, whether loving yourself by getting dressed or loving your clothes by organizing them to your content. Bottom line. Enjoying your closet is vital to your morning experience, and with only a few small updates you can you change a drab closet to an energetic one. Let's start with one of my favorite topics: color expression!

Organizing your closet by category and color is one of the easiest ways to make your styling more creative and inviting. Categorize and color coordinate everything! Start with organizing all your tops with your tops, pants with pants, dresses with dresses, skirts with skirts, jackets with jackets, and so on. Then, within each category, colorize each section by starting with black on the left-hand side and moving into browns, grays, purples, blues, greens, yellows, oranges, reds, pinks, blushes, nudes, creams, and whites (or whatever color pattern feels inspiring to you). Trust me: this is one of the most eye-pleasing ways to see your closet! And it makes getting creative in your closet so much easier.

For one, you can see what you have. You may just rediscover that favorite top of yours in bright green, which you completely forgot you owned, in the back of your closet, where it hasn't seen the light of day in a year. Oops! Poor neglected top no more. Now you can wear it! *Yay!* And two, you can also see what you are missing! Is your closet full of black tops? Or only pants and no skirts? Or perhaps your neutral-tone jackets don't spark your excitement anymore. You closet will reveal it all. Take note, and you'll know exactly what should be next on your shopping list to continue to brighten up your closet and inspire your style.

Organizing your closet with color expression makes pulling your colorful and creative items out to style each day much more effortless. They are right there waiting to be pulled! Styling made easy! Brought to you by your very own closet.

Because your closet is more than just your clothes, let's keep going, starting with your hangers. It's officially time to ditch all those dry-cleaning hangers, bulky white plastic hangers, store hangers, and any other kind of hangers that you have collected. Switch them out for slim felt hangers. Choose a single neutral color, like black or tan, so that everything feels clean and simplified. Go for white felt if you want to brighten a darker space. This kind of closet configuration makes your clothing, not the clutter, the main focus. Plus, the slim hangers will give your closet a little more room (and that means more room for new clothes), and the consistency will make it feel less chaotic. Oh hey, lower morning stress levels!

Next, it's all about the lighting! Ever put on an outfit, headed out the door, and realized that your jacket and your slacks were entirely two different shades of black? And it took stepping outside to see that they didn't match at all? Bad lighting is a big culprit for wardrobe mishaps. Not only does light bring literal energy into the space, but it also helps you see what you own. I mean, how can you see all your wonderful clothes if you can barely see at all? Bad lighting will completely ruin a closet experience. Think of the whispers! *"Did she get dressed in the dark today?"* Why yes. Yes, she did. Dim lighting can easily affect how you see your style as well as your energy level while you do it. Look to investing in better, more vibrant lighting (i.e., ditch the yellow bulbs for white ones) or even get those battery-operated lights that stick right onto the walls. It will literally and figuratively brighten your wardrobe experience with the flip of a switch.

A favorite organization method of mine is to style a shelf with chic accessories displayed for yourself. Whether inside your closet or on a bookshelf, a nearby dresser, a desk, or even a side table, any surface where you can see and enjoy them is the perfect place. There you can display some of your beloved items—earrings, scarves, bangles, et cetera—or even switch them out to new favorites as your mood so desires. Pick up some pretty jewelry organizers so you can show off your favorite pieces. Anything from clear trays for your bangles, to painted cork boards with pins to hang your necklaces on, to a stand-up mini rack for your earrings. Throw up a mirror or some wall decals behind the shelf or table, or wallpaper the back wall of the closet. Then continue to add more dimensions of your personality to your space. Or don't! Whatever inspires you most. This extension of your closet is meant to inspire you continuously, almost as if when you get dressed you are walking into your own personal store full of the items you love and shopping your own closet. And soon, oh-so soon, you will understand why seeing your accessories and making them accessible is essential to your everyday style.

Don't think I forgot about your shoe piles that accumulate day after day. In my single days, I was known to take some of my beloved shoes that I didn't wear as often and display them around the house. If I wasn't going to wear them often, at least I could look at them and remind myself I was a badass! But let's get back in the closet. We must manage the clutter so that we feel clearheaded and creative when we get dressed each day. One way is to lay out your shoes in color order. Pair all the like colors together on their rows, shelves, or across the floor. Plus, there are so many space-saving storage options too—from hanging door racks and pockets to creative cabinets to simple shelving. That way, you can see your shoes and even encourage yourself to try a new, unexpected pair on any given day. *Seeing is styling!* If you can see it, you will style it. So pull out those precious puppies and start styling more creatively.

Undoubtedly, self-care is so important to your overall style health. It's the love and attention you and your body deserve. The more you do it, the greater the benefits, not just for your style but for your life. There is nothing more empowering than knowing you are taking care of yourself and putting yourself first. It feels good! Making those kinds of decisions for yourself doesn't just inspire, it supports your feeling of ownership of your beautiful self. Keep filling up that personal love cup and you'll be shining with every step.

so, let's recap!

- Style is an act of self-care. Self-care is an act of self-love. Self-love is an act of style.

- Reconnecting to your body is an underutilized energy source for your self-love and your style expression. By loving the skin you are in, you create blossoming magnetic energy in your life and in your style.

- Don't neglect your beauty regimen. That is an act of self-care too! Taking those few extra minutes to finish off your outfit with your personal skincare, makeup, and a hairstyle that makes you happy transforms your outfit into the total look. These finishing touches support your confidence, your skin, your wardrobe, and, most importantly, your self-love.

- Your closet should be a place that inspires you, not one that overwhelms you. Organizing, stylizing, and maintaining your style sanctuary is not only an act of self-care, it also makes for a less stressed morning.

style statement

I honor myself by making acts of self-care a priority. The more self-love I give to myself and my body, the more love I bring into this world.

the style survival guide

CHAPTER 6

the truth about fit

"WHAT'S WRONG WITH MY BODY?" NOTHING!

I can't even begin to tell you how many magazines I have read over the years explaining how to dress for your body type. More recently, it's not just magazines telling women how to dress; it's websites, blogs, infographics, and social media. There is so much information out there about dressing for your body type. *Too much!* As we now know, the more we continue to collect and keep these rules in our back pockets, the harder it is to make the best style decisions for ourselves. The barrage of excessive, and sometimes conflicting, information can fog up our thinking and leave us feeling like throwing our hands up in defeat. Spoiler alert: you can just throw all of those what-you-should-wear-for-your-body-type rules out the window with the rest of the fashion rules. This is your clean slate, remember? You can reframe your thinking, which means, together, we get to re-educate you and train your mind to see style, wardrobe, and most, importantly, yourself differently.

Here is the truth about fit: there is absolutely a science for how to flatter the figure. The good news is, it's *not* rocket science! It's more like supportive guidelines for you to be creative, to own your body as it is today, and to find confidence in your clothes and your outfit choices going forward. *Fit* is actually your first lesson in what to wear. Never will I be a stylist who says you have to wear a certain type of clothing to be stylish. Instead, I am more inclined to tell you that once you master your perfect *fit*, your style becomes timeless! Yes! It's absolutely true. When your wardrobe fits you perfectly it doesn't matter what the item is you are wearing, whether it's expensive or inexpensive, whether you've had it for years or it is brand new. Having clothes that fit and flatter your figure can physically and instantly shift your perspective on your style.

It's important to be aware that the *fit* we choose to wear directly affects how we see our bodies. It is kind of like every mirror is a funhouse mirror: what your actual body shape *is* and what you *see* as your body shape are two different things. Here's a wild statistic: one hundred percent of my clients have an area of their bodies they wish could be different. Their ankles are too wide, their arms are too big, their middle is too round, their shoulders are too pronounced, their hips are too large, and the list goes on. I have something too! (Don't think for a minute I am excluded from this statistic.) For me, well . . . I could list a few things. I've always felt challenged by my high hip-bone structure. It gives me a really high hipline, which means I am super prone to muffin top. *Yay!* I have always had a love-hate relationship with my midsection. My curvy frame means clothes don't just magically fit me right off the rack. Oh, and I'm short too!

One of my more challenging personal gripes is that clothes don't seem to fit me the same way they look and fit on other people. Ever have *that* notion? It's frustrating! The collision of insecurities and negative body conversations you have with yourself as you get dressed diminishes the light inside you. Learning to flatter your figure and work with your body type is the number one tool to fight off those feelings and support you in feeling great about your body as it is today.

Did you know wearing the wrong size and the wrong fit can make you appear wider and larger than you are? Sit with that for a minute. I once had a client who absolutely hated her legs. She thought they were thick, chunky, and stubby. So she always wore really wide trouser pants and baggy jeans because, to her, those were the right items to hide her legs. If she had big legs, then she needed to wear big pants, right? *Wrong!* The wider and bigger the pant she wore, the wider her legs looked and the shorter she appeared overall. This applies to basically any area of the body. If you are trying to hide away your "problem areas," you may actually be drawing more attention to them! This is a big reason why I want you to read this book with a clean slate in your mind about what is possible for you. The reality is that when you want to minimize the appearance of something or lengthen an area, adding more fabric, more bulk, or more width to your look is only going to work against you, not for you.

Why is flattering your figure important in the first place? How you see yourself in the mirror is a key factor that informs you on what you should wear each day. By wearing clothes that flatter your true, natural, and current figure, you are using the best line of defense for that mental body-dysmorphia game we play. You are shifting the visual and mental paradigm that comes with the morning process. It's like a Jedi mind trick. If you wear clothes that are made for your frame and feature your best assets, and you see yourself in the mirror in that manner, then your mind begins to truly see it. It's a very different vision than when you are constantly looking in the mirror in ill-fitting clothes and thinking there is something wrong with you! But by using the right tools and tips for you, you are literally muscle training your brain to see yourself as the beauty you already are.

We have tricked ourselves into being blind to our beauty in the mirror. We see our negative aspects, the areas we'd like to change or hide, and the painful insecurity that comes with not fully loving our bodies the way they are. By dressing for your body, enhancing your natural beauty, and accentuating your figure and features, you are going to not only *see* yourself differently over time, you may *feel* differently about yourself too. Insecurities begone! Especially when you know that what you are wearing highlights the beautiful you. It's a much better way to experience your morning than hiding yourself under your clothes. The goal here is to teach you how to dress to feel empowered—not to feed your insecurities.

UNDERSTANDING YOUR SHAPE

When I studied image consulting at the Fashion Institute of Technology in New York City, I learned all about body shapes, which was part of why I loved the specialty. There truly is a science behind the tools you are taught. For each individual body shape, there is a set of rules that one must follow to flatter the figure. While I'm not a girl to follow the rules, I do think the guidelines for each body type are important to learn and to follow. Our bodies take all different kinds of shapes over the course of our lives, and when you know this hidden wisdom to wardrobe, your style will always be timeless. There is a harsh truth about *fit*. It's more common than not that you are wearing the wrong fit. And more importantly, and detrimentally so, you are basing that perceived "best fit" on your own personal view of your body, not the science of your actual shape. Identify your *actual* shape to educate yourself on how to flatter that beautiful figure of yours, and from there build more self-love as you continue to honor your body and yourself by wearing what makes you shine.

FIT

Fit is very simple, and once you understand the basics, you'll always be well equipped to make the best outfit decision to flatter your figure and have the opportunity to be creative with your style. From this point forth, I'd like you not to look at anything as a *rule*, but more as a *guideline* and means of education that you can work with exactly as is or change, update, or elaborate on as it suits you best, especially when it comes to body types.

Let's start with breaking down the basic body "types." For years we have been pumped with the idea that our body shape should fit into a fruit-and-veggie basket! You are an apple, a pear, a carrot, a string bean, or a peanut. Or perhaps you've been told that you were perfect for geometry class with your shape. The terms *hourglass, figure eight, triangle, inverted triangle, rectangle,* or *oval* come to mind. These are the basics that everyone uses when explaining the body types. However, you are none of those things. You don't belong in a fruit basket, and you definitely don't belong perpetually in your nightmare ninth-grade geometry class. I want you to learn the various body shapes with a new frame of mind. Read through them all, see that there is a much easier way to identify with each, and then decide where you may fit in.

- Balanced

- A little more on the top

- A little more on the bottom

- A little more in the middle

- Straight up and down

This is the science! Let's start with *balanced* because it plays a key factor in all the shapes. You've heard before that the "hourglass" is the ideal shape for a woman. Well, you can just chuck that term out the window with the rest of that old-style guidance. Let's reframe the idea of an hourglass shape to the term *balanced*. A balanced body means the width from shoulder to shoulder and the width from hip to hip are about the same measurement across. The next feature of a balanced body shape is that the waist tapers in. You can see why they would call it an hourglass. It makes sense. An alternative view of the balanced shape is if you are busty with a tapered waist and a proportionally sized derriere, creating a balanced feel to your form.

Knowing what makes a *balanced* silhouette is a vital part of everyone's style education for all shapes, balanced or not. Being balanced in your body shape flatters the figure. So, while you may have a body type that is unbalanced, your goal is to style yourself to create balance in your shape. And that is another truth about fit. Once you learn how to balance, it doesn't matter what you wear, you will have mastered the art of your own frame, instantly elevating your look and adding confidence to your vibe.

Now, balanced bodies come in all sizes. They can be a size 4 or 24. Not surprisingly, many women think they may carry their weight in the middle but in actuality they are balanced. Regardless of your actual weight or your numerical dress size, keep that in mind! The most important thing you can do as a balanced body is to define your waist! That can be in your garment structure, with a belt, or from the outline of a structured jacket. It's a simple trick that packs a body-balancing punch. The biggest balancing challenge this body shape faces is accidentally unbalancing the frame. If you style yourself with too much accentuation on either your shoulders or your hips, you can disrupt that balance. The trick here is to have your wardrobe lie close to your natural shape, with waist definition as the key ingredient. I always say if you can pinch more than an inch, either under the arms, at the chest, or in the thigh, then the pieces may be too wide for you.

Now let's say you carry your weight a little more on the bottom half—or as Beyoncé would say, "My body too bootylicious for ya, babe!" When you measure across your hipline, your hips measure wider than the measurement you take from shoulder to shoulder. The waist will taper in here as well. With this body type, the first thing you want to consider is balance. How can you rebalance your body shape? The trick is to maintain your hipline in its slimmest state with a tailored, structured, or fitted item. Then focus in on your narrow waist by defining it in some way, while adding volume or accentuation to your shoulder line. You can do that with horizontal stripes, bold colors, bright patterns, halter tops, skinny straps, and sharp shoulder points. Easy, right?

What if you have a little more on the top? This body type is usually seen as a more athletic build as it's recognized by a wider shoulder and a slimmer hip. We typically measure across the shoulder to identify this, but for women who are busty with a slim hip, this may also be where your frame lands when learning to flatter your figure.

Say it with me: "Our first step is . . . balance!" With a little more on the top half, you will want to keep your shoulder line as it is by wearing garments with a seam that sits right on your shoulder and not a centimeter past. (This technique also has a slimming effect on your frame.) Jacket fit is of utmost importance to you, and I always recommend going a size down in jackets to give yourself the slimmest look. Avoiding excess shoulder details is also a great style tactic. If you are a little bigger on top, epaulettes (shoulder tabs), and flap pockets are not your friends. Next, you'll need to define your waist and add some attention or volume to your hipline with full skirts, peplum tops, bright colors, pleats, and patterns.

What if you carry your weight in the middle? This can be a challenge for a lot of women because to flatter the figure one has to minimize the midsection and yet define the waist at the same time. *Hold up, Laurie. How can you define the waist if there isn't a waist to define?* Well, let me share the answer with you: We ALL have a waistline. But it may not be exactly where you think it is. I can tell you, for sure, it is NOT the circumference at your belly button line.

In conjunction with defining the waist, we want to make sure we maintain the natural shape of your body everywhere else. You shouldn't be stuffing yourself into tight clothing or hiding yourself in oversized or exaggerated clothing either. Instead, you should have clothing that fits and sits exactly as your body is shaped. You can utilize structure, shape, and seaming details to sharpen your frame while defining your waist to show off your balance. You can also work with your frame by using colors and lines to effectively trick the mind's eye to see your slimmest, most flattered frame. An easy base is to start with wearing the same color head to toe, such as pairing a blue blouse and a medium to dark jean together. Layer over that a brighter-colored or white jacket with structure and waist definition. This will not only support creating your balanced body, but the vertical lines of the brighter jacket against the darker base layer elongates and slims the frame too!

Now, what about a straight frame? This body type is identified by its more angular, narrow, and linear look. The shoulders and the hips may be the same distance apart, but the key factor is that the torso is mostly straight up and down. The secret to balancing here is to create the silhouette of a balanced frame through the art of how you dress. You can do this with soft, draped fabrications over the shoulders and hips paired with some form of waist definition. A wrap dress, a fit-and-flare dress, and even a structured blazer with a full skirt will support and flatter the straight frame shape.

And there you have it! This is your basic *fit* knowledge to build your style on. Keep in mind, every body is different. No body frame is exact, and there are still factors that will continue to play into your style. Whether you are short waisted or long waisted, whether you are tall or petite, whether you have long legs or a broad back, all of these aspects of your individual body make for a unique style formula that is *fit* for you. Literally and figuratively. And because you are an open information sponge, absorbing all the new information you can take, it's worth playing around with different ways to balance your shape and see what feels good. You'll know when you see it because it will feel different. Promise.

Considering there are so many variables that can affect your individual style formula, let's look at some of the basics to help you better balance, better style, and better define your frame in a way that feels good to you.

PROPORTION

The concept of proportion is an important one as it can instantly change a garment in your wardrobe from feeling heavy and weighted to feeling light and lean. Here's what you need to know: where the hemlines and seams of your wardrobe sit on you REALLY matter—imperatively so! Does your pant seam hit you in a funny place? Or does your skirt seam appear to widen your legs? Perhaps the seam placement in one of your dresses always makes you think something is off.

Here is what you should look out for: hemlines or seams should never hit you at the widest points of your body. Let's take the hips for example. A jacket or blouse hem that hits right at the hip will make you appear wider at that point, only accentuating your widest area. Tops and jackets should NEVER be worn at the widest point of your hips. It's a double whammy if your top and jacket are the same hem length, widening your appearance even further. You want to find jackets that will sit either below the widest point of your frame, like an anorak or a cargo jacket, or above that point, like a cropped denim jacket or motorcycle jacket. Bonus points for jackets that are cropped to your waist or higher. This proportion supports the lengthening of your frame and is a great tactic for petite women to use to look taller. The idea of proportion also extends to pants and skirts hems. For example, when hems hit us at the widest point of our calves, it will make our legs and our overall frames look wider and shorter. For the most flattering fit, pant and skirt hems must land at the smallest point of your legs: above the knee, below the knee, and at the ankle.

before   *after*

The idea with wardrobe and working with proper proportion is that we can utilize it to support our appearance as well as our confidence. I'm petite, and I love being petite, but it always makes me feel more fabulous when I look longer and leaner in my wardrobe, even if I'll never be taller than five feet six with heels.

MINIMIZING

Another key technique to balancing out the body frame is minimizing the widest area. You can do this with color, vertical patterns, textures, and silhouette. While, yes, darker colors minimize, by no means should you assume that means to wear black. Black is a part of this color family but not the only one. Your "darker" color could even be cobalt blue; when paired with a brighter color like white or a bold pattern, it becomes the darker color. It's crucial to never put yourself or your wardrobe into a box when it comes to playing with color. You can try anything from navy to cobalt, burgundy wine to ruby, brown to mustard, hunter green to teal. The idea is to minimize the attention to the area while keeping that area looking and feeling slim.

Silhouette is also vital to minimizing. Typically, slimmer silhouettes and/or tailored pieces will support minimizing an area of the body. As I mentioned earlier, the bulkier the garment, the more bulk is added to the look of your frame. Conversely, the closer something fits to the body, the slimmer you will appear. But let's get real here: slim doesn't necessarily mean tight, it just means tailored to the frame. Details in your garments can also help minimize areas you don't want to draw attention to. Vertical seam details, racer stripes, strategic color blocking, and pin tucks are all useful style tools as well! Just think, *Lean and lengthened, slim and structured.*

ACCENTUATING

Accentuating is the art of utilizing bright colors, bold patterns, and exaggerated details to draw attention to an area of interest. Unlike for minimizing, we want wardrobe pieces that have a little volume to them. Accentuate your shoulders with jackets with stronger shoulder points, halter tops, and off-the-shoulder necklines. A bateau neck works here too. Accentuate your hips with full skirts, bold colors, big patterns, and anything in the white/cream family.

And good news: horizontal stripes officially become your best friend here! Stripes are a great way to accentuate and widen an area you are looking to balance. A stripe on the top half of the body will widen the bustline and shoulder frame, while stripes on the bottom half of the body will widen the hip. From an overall style standpoint, accentuating is one of my strategic styling tricks. Bold necklaces will accentuate your neckline, smile, and face, while a bright, patterned, or edgy shoe will accentuate the legs, ankle, and feet. I use this style trick all the time! When I wear these accentuating details, I know attention is being drawn away from areas I am working to minimize (read: the areas of my body I don't currently love). This is why statement necklaces and bold shoe choices are always one of my go-to styling tools. Now they can be yours too!

SILHOUETTE

The term *silhouette* simply refers to the outline of a garment and the shape it creates. Silhouette is something you should always keep in mind when styling as some silhouettes can help and others can hurt you. Knowing the silhouettes that work best for your frame makes shopping and getting dressed much easier. It also can be a confidence booster, especially when the silhouette you are wearing really flatters your figure and you can *see* it!

A classic example of a silhouette gone wrong is a draped blouse. Everyone has one or something like it in their closet. For many women, they just wear it untucked, unbelted, and flowing around their hips. I mean, that *is* the silhouette it was designed with. But if you notice, blouses like that can make you feel boxy, bulky, and wide. The issue is, especially for women with a bigger bustline, the fabric will lie flat to the bust and then flow straight down from there, skipping over your waist entirely! This can absolutely change the proportion and the silhouette of your frame, essentially hiding your body. This is a classic silhouette mistake I see happen over and over again. I always joke with clients, "Like, what are you hiding under there?!" What they are actually hiding, unbeknownst to them even, is their female form! But there is an easy fix: tuck the blouse into a pencil skirt or a full skirt, wear it with a belt, half tuck it into a jean, or even wear a structured jacket over it so that the jacket frame becomes the dominant silhouette.

Let's start off small. The easiest lesson here is to start with a fit-and-flare dress shape as it is the ultimate body-balancing, female-silhouette-creating garment out there. And the best part is that it suits all body types! It's the perfect silhouette when you are first learning how to flatter your frame. Fit-and-flare dresses create the silhouette of a balanced frame. So, whether you have a little extra shoulder, a little extra hip, or even a little extra in the middle, this silhouette is going to show off your beautiful female form, without you having to try and, most importantly, without you having to hide.

So, how do you put this all together? Well, it's time to play in your wardrobe. You'll never know unless you try, and you'll be surprised the difference you will see in your overall look, even with the smallest of updates or changes. For example, maybe you absolutely *love* big, bold-printed tops but you also have a bigger bustline. Try switching those prints to your bottoms and see what happens. Maybe you carry a little more in the middle and you are also petite. Try layering a fitted denim jacket over a look you typically would wear and then cuff up your sleeves. Maybe you love black but have a broader shoulder. Try a more voluminous skirt in a black lace so that you are still honoring your style but adding in a silhouette and noticeable texture to accentuate your hipline. The idea here is that you now get to try out at home all the different ways to balance your frame and visually see your body. But before you jump into your closet, there is one more very important style tool that is going to become your best styling friend, now and always.

DON'T WASTE YOUR WAIST

Other than *balance, balance, balance,* did you notice a common denominator in all the tips to flattering the different body types? In my work, it is the most important piece to the puzzle. It's the number one thing you should consider when styling yourself, creating a flattering outfit, and building confidence. To me, this is the key that will change your life. *I swear! No, really! I'm not kidding!* This is the one thing that will change your life, change how you style yourself, and, most importantly, change how you feel about yourself. Are you ready?

Define *your* waist.

Before I get to the why, do you even know where your waist is? Like, your real waist. Not your waist where your jeans make muffins. Not the waist where your belly button lives. Not the waist that you don't think you even have in the first place! I'm talking about your actual waistline. The waistline that helps you create your balance body. The waist that is the slimmest point of your frame. The High Waist. (*Ahhhh!* Cue church choir!)

Every time I do a style talk for women, I always have my ladies stand up and put their hands in superhero pose where they think their waist is. Consistently, every single time, every woman puts her hands on her high hips.

"Okay, and let's move your hands higher."

And they will inch up their hands.

Again I say, "Higher!" and with confused looks on their faces, they inch their hands higher.

Finally I say, "Okay. Now one last time! Just a little higher so you are actually above your belly button!"

Everyone looks at me with such astonishment. You can read their faces like a book. "Wait, my waist is not around the middle? My waist is all the way up here near my boobs?"

My answer? Yes! This is your high waist! It's that little special sweet spot between your belly button and your bustline. It's right around where your two lowest and detached ribs are located. Believe it or not, this is the slimmest part of your body. This is officially your high waist, and this goes for all body shapes.

Why is this important? Because the waist is not only at the center of your body balance, it's also at the center of your empowerment. A couple of things happen when you define your waist. Not only do you flatter your figure to support the balance of your body, but you also lengthen your frame. This effect happens when you define your high waist, creating the illusion of a longer leg line. Now, as we know, everybody is different, so exactly where that perfect sweet spot is for you is going to be a little different from body to body.

So, let's find yours. Stand up and put your hands at your high waist. Then move your hands around to find where that spot is for you. It's about two inches above your belly button and two inches below your bustline. Because you may not be used to this spot as a focal point for your body, it may feel awkward for you. And if it feels really awkwardly high and you think to yourself, *That can't be my waist!* then you've found it! Good job!

Now you can define your waist in all sorts of ways. You can add a belt to basically any outfit—over a dress, over a blouse, or over a jacket, if you want to try that style out for yourself (I'm all for creative style, you know).

You can define your waist by wearing a dress that has a center waist-panel built into it. You can define your waist by wearing a fit-and-flare dress. Hey, why not throw a belt on top of that while you're at it? You can also define your waist by wearing a tailored jacket that has built-in waist definition. Blazer doesn't suit you? (Oooh, a style pun!) Try a casual cargo jacket that has a toggle at the waistline. That way, you can gather up the jacket, creating a fit-and-flare effect.

How about wearing a high-waisted pencil skirt? (This styling tactic is a personal favorite of mine, and it works wonders!) There is a big misconception about pencil skirts and skirts in general. Almost every closet that I have been in had skirts that were too big. Believe or not, I always recommend trying a size down when you buy your skirts. The reason is because at your regular size the skirt will fit perfectly at your belly button. This positioning is not necessarily the most flattering place for the skirt to sit, and many women then get scared of wearing skirts because of that. I recommend going a size down so that your skirt zips up at the high waist, above your belly button. Why is that a great way to style? Because when you wear a pencil skirt at the high waist, not only does it define your waist, it acts as a girdle to your midsection. Tuck in your blouse and you have the ultimate figure-flattering outfit. Hey, while you're at it, you might as will put a belt on top of it too!

No matter your body shape, defining your

waist is a consistent tool that you can always use to help you flatter your figure and look balanced, longer, leaner, and slimmer. And most importantly, it will support you in feeling more confident as a woman.

BREAKING THROUGH BODY BARRIERS

While these body guides won't ever change, your body will. It will change through the years in ways that you couldn't have imagined. From hormones to pregnancies to menopause, many things cause the female figure to change. So, while your body may go through changes, you can rest assured that these tips will always be something you can go back to to support your mind and your body by acknowledging where you are and then pulling out the styling tools to flatter your figure, no matter its shape.

One of the biggest body challenges often comes from pregnancy and having babies. After children, your body changes significantly, but so does your life. As a woman, you become the last priority. You put your career, your husband, your kids, the family pet, and everyone else before you. (This also happens so often to girl-bosses.) Being the last priority can weigh on you. When you aren't taking care of you, you tend to lose sight of how to do so. You find less and less time for self-care and find more and more excuses as to why you can't make a change at this point. Trust me, I've heard it all!

Savannah's is one of those stories. Savannah came to me because she had lost touch with herself. With a full-time career, a husband, and three children, she had a full plate. She was a dedicated mother and the matriarch of her family, a busy professional and wife. Yet day in and day out she was getting up, throwing on old maternity clothes, tossing her coat over it all to hide herself, and heading out the door. She was uninspired and lost and didn't even know where to begin.

The first thing I noticed in her closet was that she hadn't shopped for herself in a very long time. The newest pieces she had had been given to her by her mom. (Moms are the best, aren't they? They always have our best interests at heart!) Her mom knew that Savannah might feel better if she just dressed a little better, so she sent her a floral pencil skirt, a striped blouse, and a few other items. As we tried on her wardrobe, I quickly discovered that most of Savannah's clothes didn't fit her well. They were made for a different body shape, and many of the items were specifically made for a pregnant figure. So here Savannah is, years later, her youngest two years old now, and she is still putting on maternity clothes and oversized wide-leg trousers with a long cardigan on top to cover her derriere and a simple black flat to walk out the door.

Something had to change. But before we were going to change her wardrobe, Savannah had to face her body. I needed her to look in the mirror and see and accept the body she had so we could discuss how to balance it and then how to style it. Together in the mirror, we went down her frame area by area. Her shoulders were broad, and after three kids her chest was buxom. Then we looked at her waist.

"There it is!" I said.

She looked at me like I was crazy, pointing to her belly button region, high hips, and hipline. "I have no waist," she said. (This literally happens every appointment.)

And in turn, I responded, "Of course you do!"

Then we evaluated her hips. Without using a tape measure, it's easy to eyeball if the shoulders and the hips are the same distance apart or not. To me they looked closely balanced, but because Savannah was more voluptuous on the top half of her frame, she fell more into the category of "carrying a little more on the top."

Our next step was to help her pull out the clothes and work on our balancing act. I loved the floral pencil that her mom purchased (thanks, Mom). While the pencil skirt kept her frame lean looking, the floral pattern drew attention down to her hips, helping to balance out her bustline. I then paired it with a heather-gray jewel-neck top. The more subdued tone and the fitted shape were meant to minimize her upper frame and follow along her natural figure. This way, the eye-catching floral skirt supported the balancing act.

Prior to this moment, she had only worn the skirt once. She would take her looser-fitting, tunic-length tops and layer them over the skirt. Then she would add a same-length cardigan with a draped front over all of that. Here's what was wrong: Savannah was hiding her waist and distorting the proportion of her body. Being that she was about average height (five feet five to five feet six), proportion really mattered for Savannah. Wearing a top that was too long in the front made her appear shorter, wider, and top-heavy, especially when she added a floaty draped cardigan on top of that. It was a perfect storm of the wrong look.

After removing the cardigan, we made only one simple change for her to see the difference. We replaced her tunic with the gray top and tucked it into her skirt.

At first she said, "I've never tucked in my shirt like this before. Are you sure I can wear it this way?"

"Of course, but it's missing one more thing," and I grabbed one of her belts that she never wore and placed it around her waistline.

When I turned Savannah toward the mirror, she just stood there and stared. Here she was, wearing a top she always wore untucked, now tucked into a pencil skirt featuring her high waist with a belt to define her waist even more. You know what she saw? Her beautifully balanced body.

She looked at me and said, "Is that my body?"

"Yes!" I said. "It is. This is your body. And now that you can see what I see, it's time for you to start dressing this beautiful body every day."

Savannah proceeded to examine herself in the mirror. "This belt really makes me look slim! And look at my curves! I didn't even think I could look that way." She started to tear up.

And I started to tear up! I always do! I treasure this part.

Savannah then lit up with possibility and said, "Wait, can I take this belt and put it over the draped cardigan?"

My answer? "Yes! Of course you can. Let's try it!"

So we took her cardigan and put it over her tucked-in blouse. Then we added the belt on top of it all! I turned her to the mirror again, and her face lit up.

She smiled and looked at me. "Oh my goodness, I cannot believe how good this looks!"

I just smiled and nodded.

I knew, of course, but this process is not about me telling you what you have to do; instead, it's about guiding you into a new light of possibility. For Savannah, that possibility was realizing there was so much more to her wardrobe than she had ever fathomed for herself. So we kept styling, we made more outfits, we layered belts, we tucked in her blouses, we made looks that she could wear to work and that she could wear as "Mom." If it supported her feeling confident and feminine and beautiful, we built it together.

A few weeks later, Savannah called me out of the blue with a wild story. While working at her desk, her close coworker came in and shut the door to her office.

She got in close and whispered in her ear, "I really need to know what's going on with you. Is something going on with you? Is there something you need to tell me? Is everything okay at home? Are you having an affair?"

And Savannah laughed out loud and said, "No, of course not! I hired a stylist!"

Seriously, this is one of my favorite success stories to date! But the truth is, it wasn't just about the stylist. The shift happened when Savannah implemented wearing clothes that flattered her figure, so when she saw herself in the mirror she saw the beautiful, alluring, empowered, and confident woman she already was. An experience with understanding her current body type and learning how to flatter it entirely changed Savannah's perspective of herself, her wardrobe, and her life.

This kind of mind and body shift reverberates in every area of your life, from your work to your marriage to motherhood. Savannah was embracing her life in a whole new light. She now remembers that she's a woman who is confident and sexy and beautiful, even after having three kids. The beautiful part about this? She never has to go back. She can always continue to build, maintain, and grow her confidence as well as her personal style.

The truth about *fit* is that you don't have to listen to anyone else ever again about what looks best on you and your current frame. With the raw knowledge of how to balance your body and how to use the tool of defining your waist, you can be the master of your own style story and body confidence. Think about it this way: dressing *as if* will lead you to actually become *it*. That is the style secret behind embracing your body, flattering your figure, and owning who you are from the inside out.

so, let's recap

- Don't let your perception of your body determine your style choices. There is a science to dressing your form and flattering your figure. Learn the science, and you'll always be able to flatter your figure no matter what shape you are.

- Don't put yourself in a fruit basket. Getting technical with your body shape can make getting dressed less personal and more strategic. Know your actual shape and you can use the tools of balance, waist definition, proportion, minimizing, accentuating, and silhouette to flatter your figure at any stage of your life.

- Defining your waist is one of the secret sauces to your empowered style. It not only supports your body balancing act, it also supports your mindset, reminding you that you are all woman. (Hear you roar, girl!)

- Tried, tested, and true: Master the fit tools for you and no matter how your body changes, you'll always be able to come back to the basics to redefine yourself, define your frame, and reveal that inner confidence.

style statement

{To be said while holding your hands in Wonder Woman pose at your high waist. Yes, your high, high waist! Chin up, girl! You got this!}

I will no longer choose to style myself in silhouettes that are not right for my shape and proportion. Instead, I will use style strategy, a little compassion, and a lot of love (and waist definition!) to flatter my figure and feel fabulous in anything I wear.

CHAPTER 7

be self-expressed

THE POWER OF SELF-EXPRESSION

Believe it or not, the Law of Attraction is a key part of why style is transformational. Not just for your closet but for your life and your soul. The Law of Attraction is simply this: the energy you put out into the world is the energy you get back. Put out negative, self-deprecating vibes, and watch as negative energy finds you. Put out positive and powerful self-love vibes, and those same vibrations attract to you like a magnet. This is the idea in its simplest form. But it matters so much as we revolutionize your morning experience so that you create more powerful energy field around yourself each and every day.

Once I worked with a client who lived in a constant state of "I can't." When Elena and I talked about her style, she couldn't bear the thought of change. She couldn't even take physical action toward trying something new. She was terrified. More than that, she felt like she was truly stuck there. And Elena submitted to being stuck. Deep down in her soul, she wanted more for herself, more for her closet, more for her life, and more for her experience with herself. But when it came down to it, she had just given up. When we hit that low mark, sometimes that hole we dig for ourselves feels impossible to climb out of. Trust me, I know. I've been there. There's nothing worse than the feeling that trying isn't worth the effort anymore because you already assume you are going to fail.

Elena kept validating her morning experience with this feeling and continuously perpetuating her future. She wasn't being recognized at work, she was unmotivated and terribly unproductive, and she felt like others at her office were surpassing her in success. Most notably, she felt like her life wasn't at all the life she wanted to be living. More than a style makeover, Elena needed a self-love makeover. Her negative experience getting dressed validated her poor sense of self.

I tasked Elena with a simple action each day to help her make baby steps to get out of the negative place she was in. One morning she had to wear a bold color, another morning it was to take an extra-long shower and do a body scrub. On the next day she had to wear something in her closet she hadn't worn before. And on the day after that, she had to style her hair differently than normal. Day by day, she did a different task. One of her tasks was to take herself shopping after work and try on something she normally would tell herself she couldn't wear. Another task was to wear a necklace she was saving for the perfect occasion on a random weekday. Each day she did something new, something different, sometimes pushing her creativity and sometimes focusing solely on her self-care and self-love.

Ultimately, the whole task list was not just an exercise in pushing her comfort zones, it was also a way of introducing more self-love and self-honor into her morning experience. Right away, Elena saw results. First and foremost, she started to feel better. She was trying new things, feeling more open to possibilities, and stepping out of her negative morning comfort zone. Second, she began to look forward to the tasks each day. It excited her! What fun, new step would she try tomorrow? Especially when it was a style challenge. On those days, she popped over her closet with delight. What outfit could she create next? Over time, Elena relied less and less on the task list, because she was finally making creative moves for herself, and she was having fun doing it. At work she was smiling more and feeling more productive, and her boss even noticed her more positive presence just while she was sitting at her desk. "Something is different about you, Elena!" Each day she took another step toward making her energy brighter and more vibrational around her.

To this day, she's evolving and taking more risks. She is traveling, found love, and is finally living the life she always dreamed of but never thought she deserved. She did deserve it. And her daily acts of self-love, creativity, and style creation were just the catalyst to light the path and show her the way.

Sometimes it takes a routine shake-up to get out of the style and mood rut you may be in. The more you explore your creativity, finding new ways and outfits to express who you are at the core, the more you manifest that creativity and expression in your overall life. This part of style acts as mental, emotional, and physical self-care as well as self-love. That is something we all need. Getting dressed and ready for the day is your time to honor who you are each and every morning. You get to say, *This is ME and today this is how I am going to define myself for the world to see.* That kind of daily morning exercise in creativity and action has a very powerful life reaction. Positive change.

OVERCOMING FEAR AND CULTIVATING CREATIVITY

How does one get creative? I know from my work with women that style creativity involves a section of the brain that needs to be retrained and educated properly. Yes, there are definitely women with innate creativity out there (and you may be one of them), but women consistently tell me that creativity in their closet is an overwhelming and impossible task. They don't see the opportunities in their wardrobe. Instead, they see singularity. For example, a printed blouse goes with solid slacks. One and done.

When I see a printed blouse I think, *Wow! Look at all the options.* A printed blouse tucks into a pencil skirt for work. It wears well with white jeans and tan wedges for brunch, or it looks great with blue jeans and a blazer for networking. It also looks cute with a striped full skirt for a Saturday girlfriend playdate, or even with a pair of shorts and gladiator sandals for a Sunday stroll. I mean, that is just off the top of my head. Think about how much more I can create when I'm in a closet! There is always so much opportunity.

Good news! This way of thinking can be taught. Creativity can be taught. Let's start with probably my signature phrase to work with when getting dressed and pushing your comfort zone. To see past what you know and explore more expressive ideas is as simple as saying, "YES! Why not?" to any idea you come up with, good or bad. Try it on and see. You never know what you'll discover! Want to try navy and mustard yellow together? Why not! Want to try a floral blouse with a red jacket? Why not! Want to try a green necklace but a gold earring? Why not! Just. Try. It. The harsh reality is you will be forever stuck if you never venture outside your box of understanding. If you never even try, you stop your creativity right in its tracks.

But why are we stopping ourselves? Sometimes it isn't just a lack of ideas, those pesky old rules, or personal perceptions that haunt us. Sometimes there is something deep going on. We've touched on it before, and it's worth mentioning again. FEAR! A fear of judgment, fear of sticking out, and fear of just being seen. I've had so many clients over the years tell me this was why they didn't dress more creatively. They were scared to stand out, to try something new, and to even just break the routine. *Darn comfort zone!* It's a very scary feeling for many to defy their fears. What if people notice me? What if people see me? What if people judge me? Those are strong feelings that can really affect how we express ourselves—not just with our clothes but how we feel about ourselves and the energy we exude.

I bet by now you are seeing why the relationship you have with yourself and your wardrobe is crucial in your life. It's incredible how many factors stall us from dressing for our best lives and, ultimately, from living our best lives. But these things are not insurmountable! Start changing up one thing a day for a week and see how you feel. It's just one small, simple thing in your wardrobe and in your routine. No pressure. No stress. You don't have to be perfect. You don't have to get it "right" every day. You just have to make the choice, then try again and again and again.

There really is something to be said for feeling like you are your best, most expressive self. It's freeing. It's powerful, it's full, and it's lively. It's letting go of those feelings that are stalling you, and allowing yourself to be anything you want to be! I mean, you literally can be *anything* you want to be, especially when it comes to your style. It is quite an empowering feeling when we can allow ourselves to just be ourselves! Style is the gateway to get you there. Stylepowerment is yours for the taking!

Here's the big question, and I want you to really sit and think about it: What would it feel like if your creativity were flowing out of you, so much so that you acted upon every new, interesting, and inspiring idea you came up with? What would you be wearing? How would you be walking? What would you be feeling? Hold on to that vision of yourself as it will fuel your next steps as you learn to spark the creativity inside of you with the easiest style tools, which you most likely already own.

THE IMPACT OF ACCESSORIES

Accessories are an integral part of your creativity. Playing with them is the perfect first lesson in how to get creative on your own. Accessories are the finishing touches to an outfit that can literally make or break your look, and they are another way to style with intention. Think about it this way: without adding intentional details (accessories) to an outfit, your outfit isn't an outfit, it is just clothing you are wearing. You can easily test this concept at home. Next time you get dressed, get your whole outfit together with no accessories and take a good look in the mirror. Now go pop on a pair of colorful earrings or a bold necklace. Hey, maybe add a belt while you're at it! Now take a second look in the mirror. Can you see the difference? Adding the accessories is like putting the cherry on top of your outfit! It sends a message too—*I have my own unique personality!*

This is probably not shocking news at all, but I *love* accessories. Since I was a little girl, I have been expressing my own unique personality with accessories. One of my most cherished necklaces ever was those colorful plastic charms on the plastic chain. You know, from the '80s? I had a hair dryer and a lipstick, a convertible car, a cassette tape, and a million more. Thanks to my mom saving all my elementary school photos, I recently was reminded that I was wearing statement necklaces before I even realized what a valuable asset they were to me. In my second-grade class picture I wore a black-and-white-striped T-shirt with a pink crew-neck collar with matching pink bike shorts (obvi!), and perfectly paired with it was a matching pink, red, blue, and green oversized button necklace. I was too cool for school!

Over the years, accessories became not just an obsession but a strategic styling tool for me and a crucial part of my original self-expression. They were my go-to pieces when I needed something more to my look, a personal pick-me-up, or just something to make me feel special. The best part about accessories for me was that for those months and years when I couldn't afford a lot of new clothing, and I still wanted to pack a stylistic punch, I would go after *all* the accessories. A simple necklace change can completely update the vibe of an outfit. And I became the master of that wardrobe transformation for myself.

Accessories were, and still are, my crowning pieces to the outfits I style to express myself. But as I developed my private personal styling business, it became increasingly clear to me how foreign accessorizing was to my clients. Something that felt like such an innate part of my creativity was a strain for others. I have had clients who literally did not own one piece of jewelry, ones who only wore the same chain necklace every day, and ones who had an overflowing drawer of jewelry, scarves, and belts but absolutely no idea what to do with them and never wore any of them. Actually, women often tell me they don't wear accessories because they just don't know what to wear or even how to wear them!

Necklaces are a great starting point when working on how to wear accessories. Here's why. A necklace can fill in the negative space of an open neckline. A necklace can frame the face so that you become the star of your look. *Hello, beautiful face!* It can also add a little color or sparkle to brighten your skin tone. If you have more mature skin around your neckline, a necklace provides quite the sleight of style act, covering up what you may not want others to focus on, while reflecting shine and framing your gorgeous face. Want me to go on? Because there is more! A necklace can help elongate your neck if you are wearing a top that is cutting you in the wrong place. A necklace also is a conversation starter. And lastly, a necklace can add dimension and personality to your outfit with the clip of a clasp. Have I made the case yet?

Now, not to fret if you are one of the many who don't have a lot of accessories to work with. And even if you do, here's my must-have checklist of items to invest in and play around with:

A statement necklace – You know, one of those necklaces that catches eyes, turns heads, and sparks a conversation. Something big, bold, colorful, sparkly, or all of the above—you pick! If you can snag even a couple of these that spark your style fancy, they will really come in handy when building your outfits from day to day.

A set of three dainty layering chains – There are necklaces that come made like this, or you can try layering some of your own dainty necklaces together to create a bigger statement. The trick is to make sure they all land at different levels around your neck and décolletage.

A pendant necklace – Think long and down the front with a large emblem at the bottom. It could be a large quartz stone on leather, or a tassel at the helm of some beautiful beads like a mala necklace, or it could be a chain with a colorful flower at the end. Whatever sparks you.

A statement earring – One of my personal favorites in my jewelry box makes a bold expression. Look for something fun and colorful. A pair of tassel earrings or oversized drops will do the trick. And the best part is, they help draw attention to your gorgeous face.

A pair of classic hoops – These are a must, but just because they are classic doesn't mean they have to be boring! You can go simple, or you can look for ones with crystals, spiked edges, mixed metals, or a small pendant that hangs from the bottom. Or choose a shape other than a circle, such as oblong hoops. I especially love the hoops that are shaped like hearts or stars. Why not!

A pair of modern stud earrings – Stash away the simple studs for now and look for modern details like arrows, hearts, clovers, pyramid spikes, or geometric shapes. Go further with wrap-around backings, or even try an ear crawler! Bonus points for extra earring holes! You can layer them and mix and match your shapes.

A set of mix-and-match bangles – To create this look you can layer together different bracelets from different sets into the same look. Try mixing metals, playing with multiple colors, and even layering with various sizes. This is a fresh and easy way to infuse the energy of fun into any look.

A set of stacking rings – I love this as an accessories option because you can either layer them all together on one finger to create one larger statement or separate them across a few fingers for a more bohemian vibe. There is nothing like versatility in your wardrobe! More creativity to be had and more bang for your buck—a double whammy in my style book!

A silk scarf – Find one in a pattern that you love and that mixes well with your wardrobe. You can wrap it around your neck, lace it through the loops of your jeans, or tie it around the handle of a handbag. You can style a beautiful head wrap with it or even just tie it around the band of your ponytail and let the corners hang down. Très chic!

A colorful or metallic skinny belt – To me, belts are the ultimate item for every wardrobe, and I go more in-depth on that soon. But for now, let's make sure you have at least the ones you need to enhance your wardrobe (and empowerment). Skinny belts can be worn at your high waist or your hipline. At the high waist it will add style to any dress, over a blouse, over a cardigan, or over a pencil skirt. At the low waist it can loop through your slacks' or denim belt loops. They add instantaneous style, intention, and dimension to every look.

Neutral-tone medium to wide belt – A must for frame-flattering magic. A wide belt can be between two and three inches wide. These are great on all frames but work their magic especially on curvy bodies with a little more in the middle, or long torsos. And they go stylishly over dresses, skirts, and even blazers for a more fashion-forward take.

An original hat – If you know me personally, you know I have a penchant for hats. Big ones, small ones, colorful ones, and yes, I have even worn printed ones. They are an instantaneous style fix for a simple outfit or a bad hair day. Having a hat that elevates your style vibe can change your look, but also how you feel about your look. Add fun, add mystery, add creativity or edge—hats do it all. Bonus: they make great conversation starters!

A pair of shoes to conquer in – Marilyn Monroe once said, "Give a girl the right shoe and she can conquer the world." There is something so powerful about putting on a shoe that empowers you. That is why it is a must for your accessory arsenal. Be bold with your shoe choice or be simple, be colorful or be sparkly, be tall in heels or comfortable in short stacks. No matter which shoe style works for you, make sure it emboldens your sense of self and allows you to step into your personal power every time you hit the pavement.

A leather handbag – This should be an obvious item on the list; however, I have discovered that the majority of women don't invest in their handbags often, if at all. Instead, they tote around the same weathered bag everywhere they go. A fresh leather bag, whether real or vegan, will update and upgrade any look—from casual to work to dressy. If it's been a while, time to treat yourself, girl! You deserve it.

The truth is, accessorizing is one of the easiest ways you can get creative while learning to exercise that style-expression muscle. With the exception of investment handbags and shoes, accessories are relatively small and easily interchangeable, and they allow so much opportunity for creativity! Let's have some fun, shall we? Head over to your jewelry and pull out all your favorite pieces, big and small, whether you wear them every day or have been "saving" them for the perfect moment. Pull them out, lay them out across your dresser or in an easily visible place, and make a point to start wearing them. It really is that simple.

Like all creative ideas with style, the most effective way to work through the feeling of "what now?" is by saying "why not!" Just try it! I always love the part when a client will spark a little lightbulb as we are discussing how to play with accessories. She'll run over to pull out this oversized statement necklace that she bought, left in a back drawer, and never once wore, and say, "Do you mean I can wear *this* necklace with *these* earrings with *this* blouse for work?" And my answer? "YES!" Then the ideas start to flow: "What about *this* hat with *this* scarf and *these* statement earrings with *this* T-shirt, torn jeans, and sneakers?" "Yes! That too!" I reply.

It's that personal style discovery process that really can break the barriers and reignite the creativity inside you. It can be a big mood changer too! Imagine how your mornings would feel if going through your jewelry box and accessory drawers were as filled with enchantment and delight as you felt when you were a child going through your mom's accessories. That alone would start your morning off on an upbeat note. Accessorizing means that every morning your wild imagination gets to come out to play.

But there is actually more to accessorizing than just its style aspect. It can shift the perception of your image. **Accessories have impact**. Accessories aren't just a way for you to express your creativity, they are a way to showcase that creativity to the outside world. By styling yourself and using accessories to really add some personality to your look, you are giving off some very important messages. **One**, you are creative! You have a mind of your own and you are not afraid to use it! **Two**, you care about your look. You took the extra time in the morning to put yourself together and add the finishing touches. It shows that your image matters to you, which will cause people to take you more seriously. And **three**, when you take the extra time with your look, give attention to the details, and then wear it confidently, it adds a powerful subconscious perception about you. If you take care of yourself this well at home, imagine the kind of work you provide at the office or with your services! Wearing your accessories, subtly or with bold abandon, shows that you are somebody who will put the finishing touches on everything you do. And *that* is somebody people can get behind.

Remember the Law of Attraction. Even spending a few extra minutes on adding the perfect finishing touch accessories to your outfit will send off new vibrational waves into the world. Accessorizing *is* self-care! Try it and watch what happens next.

CREATIVITY THROUGH COLOR

Wearing color is another simple and obvious form of creativity that has even more of an impact on your outfit, style, and—get this—your mood too! Add a pop of color to a simple look and it instantaneously energizes the outfit. Yet I've worked with so many women who were timid when it came to color. *What if I stand out? What if it doesn't look right? Is this the right color for me?* I completely understand those fears, but I am going to dish you some major color truth right now. Then I'm going to tell you exactly how to style color for yourself.

First, let's get something out of the way. Have you ever been told you're a Summer? Or an Autumn? When it comes to wearing colors, there are image consultants who specialize in color analysis and will drape you in color after color to help you determine whether you are a Spring, Summer, Autumn, or Winter. I'm trained in this skin tone analysis too. However, in my personal styling work, I have found that fitting my clients into a "season" never felt right. Instead, it felt limiting, overwhelming, and very confusing for my clients when they did actually go out shopping with their

swatches. In the end, it can bring up more questions about what you should purchase than it gives answers.

Even though I love color and color education, this system didn't fit my styling formula, and, most importantly, it didn't fit the lifestyle of my clients. They didn't want to fit into a box of colors. They wanted freedom to express their colorful desires without feeling concerned that they were doing something wrong or against their palette. Just like flattering your figure, there is a science to the colors that look best on us. For each of our individual skin, eye, and hair colorations and combinations there is a specific saturation, intensity, vibrancy, and undertone of colors that are a perfect match for our unique selves. But you don't need a set of swatches to dictate what colors you can use to express yourself. Rather, there are some really simple guides to get you started and help you find your personal creativity.

The color-swatch method teaches you whether you have a warm, cool, or neutral undertone, as well as whether you look better in dustier colors versus more saturated colors, and there are so many variations in between. The simplest way to get a handle on your undertone is to put on some jewelry! Ask yourself this: Do I look better in gold jewelry or in silver jewelry? (Disclaimer: this doesn't mean you can't wear both!) It's definitely noticeable to see when gold glows on you versus when silver glows on you. If it's gold, you are a warm undertone. If it's silver, you are a cool undertone. If both look fantastic on you, then you may be a neutral. Pretty easy, right?

Now, what does that mean? It means that wearing colors that match your undertone will definitely look better on you. However, don't get caught in a black-or-white kind of thinking about it all. Just because you may be a warm undertone doesn't mean you are stricken to wear dark brown for the rest of your life. That just sounds awful. You can totally wear black! Break those rules, girl. The trick is to make sure you layer in other colors that glow for you. Maybe you add a scarf with some jewel tones over a black blouse. Or maybe your necklace has gold in it to punch up the brightness of your face. **You don't have to be perfect, and you don't have to get it right every time.** What you can do is start with a new awareness of yourself and your wardrobe, which will help you spice up your style, your mood, and your life.

Want to know how you can really tell what colors have the right undertone for you? You can tell by just looking in the mirror. Have you ever put a color on and said, "YIKES! That looks terrible on me"? Hey! Good news: you are right! Trusting your gut is your internal first line of defense when it comes to discovering the colors that are right for you. You should only be wearing what makes your skin glow. And trust me, it's definitely something you can absolutely see in the mirror.

You know what else makes your skin glow? Brighter colors, jewel tones, and colors that make you smile. While some skin tones do look harmonious with dim, moody color tones, I have found that, no matter the age or "season" of my client, the more bright colors and saturated tones she integrates into her wardrobe, the brighter and more youthful her skin appears. It's true! Plus, brighter and more saturated colors add vibrancy, youth, and energy to your look. They also raise your personal vibration, and your magnetism too. I mean, who doesn't want that? Try it for yourself! You've got this, and this is a perfect place to start exploring what feels good for you as you continue shifting your personal style perspective. The wardrobe you wear should always make you twirl, dance around, or walk with a strut from the moment you put it on. Imagine if all the clothes you wore made you feel that way. *Why would you wear anything else?* Just sayin'.

So how can we break through the fear of wearing color? The surprising thing about color is that adding it into your wardrobe is as easy as just wearing it! It's that creativity blocker in your mind that says, "No, not today," that stops us on our style path and veers us back into what is comfortable and dark and hides who we are. In light of that, I want you to reframe your thinking about color.

What if all colors—bold or soft, light or dark—were considered a neutral tone, with the same styling and color-combination power as neutrals, like black, camel, gray, white, cream, khaki, tan, and brown? What would you do with it then? How would you wear it? How would you pair it? Breaking this color barrier is important because if you instantly say to yourself, "No, that doesn't work," without even trying it out to see, you'll never know the possibilities in store for you! So what's my mantra here? Should you try it? YES! Why not? Go for it. Playing with color should be fun, fearless, and imaginative. Once you break through that personal barrier that is holding you back, there is a whole closet of color, energy, and potential waiting for you.

YES. YOU. CAN.

Yes. You. Can. It really is that simple. And it all starts with my trademark saying: "YES! Why not?" Just try it. Maybe it doesn't work, and that's okay. You experimented creatively, and that practice of experimentation is an essential tool to breaking your previous style patterns. But maybe, just maybe it works. And what if it works so well that it's literally a life changer? Now you are fueling your soul with creative ideas, the power of *yes*, and a whole new style story that you get to write for yourself.

See a dress in a store window and think, *Wow, that is so beautiful?* Go try it on! Pull out that top you were saving for a special occasion but are secretly considering for your next Monday meeting. Absolutely wear it! See some inspiration on Pinterest that you love? Go find similar pieces in your closet and see if you can recreate the vibe! The bottom line here? Go for it! The only person stopping you from embracing and enjoying your personal style experience is you.

Maya Angelou said, "You can't use up creativity. The more you use, the more you have." And it is so true. The more you introduce fun to your style, the more fun you will have with your style! Own that and you won't just be constantly growing and evolving, but you will be making a statement about who you are each and every day. I am me! I am creative! And I am going to shine today! Sounds like a nice title for a style story, doesn't it?

so, let's recap!

- Shaking up your current style automation is one of the easiest ways to explore new possibilities in your creativity. The more you explore your creativity, the more you set the stage and tone to shape the newly style-empowered world around you.

- Seeking your own unique sense of creativity means letting go of the fear that holds you back, saying, "No, that won't work for me." We stop ourselves before we even start, and it is officially time to begin.

- Accessorizing is one of the easiest ways to get your creative juices flowing. Adding accessories to your outfit adds personality, creativity, dimension, and detail. Bonus: Accessorizing is fun!

- Color is creativity. The more color you can play around with and incorporate into your outfits, the brighter, more positive, and more vibrant you will look and feel.

- Self-expression is a muscle that you can strengthen with the power of yes! Be open to your creativity. Say "Yes! Why not?" when trying out new ideas. This fresh way of thinking and styling can open new doors, new opportunities, and new vibrations in your closet and in your life.

style statement

I am not afraid to express the truest and brightest me, from the inside out. I am going to explore new, creative style enhancements, like playing with color and accessories, to help build my personal style-expression muscle.

game-changing style tools

DRESSING WITH INTENTION

Have you heard of the new trend "laissez chic"? Oh, no? Well, of course you haven't; I made it up! It's my answer to many of my clients' most sought-after question: "How can I have *style* if I am totally lazy?" I love this question, and I get it often.

So, what is "lazy" as it pertains to your style? Are you too lazy to make an effort, too lazy to try, too lazy to do anything different than you've done before? Or perhaps it's too lazy to make the time. And, girl, that really does affect everything else in your life. Your style is part of your self-care, and lazy style means you are not taking care of yourself properly. The unfortunate truth is that it shows in your clothes. This is a very real issue! By no means are we lazy, but we definitely can feel that way. The reality? We women are movers and shakers, and by the time we finally get to taking care of ourselves, we tend to throw our hands up and give up. Our experience leaves us feeling like we cannot even fathom putting any more effort into ourselves. In the end, we become lazy about doing the things that service our soul, all the while putting 150 percent into others.

We lean into being "lazy" in our style when we feel *style* is difficult. We see others looking put-together and question how they do that, while doubting our own ability to do the same. Instead of being inspiring, *style* feels overwhelming, and getting dressed can feel like an absolute chore.

My client Marissa was one of those women who had hit that wall and hit it hard. She's a single mom who traveled for work with a hyper-conservative work wardrobe of classic shift dresses in solid colors, structured tote handbags, and basic pumps. Yet at home she aspired to be her true self, a bohemian rock goddess with a wild side. When it came time for Marissa to dress casually, she reverted to a pair of worn tennis shoes, unflattering shorts, and a T-shirt.

When I arrived at her closet, I discovered it was full of super colorful and playful casual clothes that really exemplified her style vision. She had fitted motorcycle jackets, fringy sweaters, cool studded belts, edgy booties, mixed-media bangles with leather and chains, stunning stone pendant necklaces in amethyst, rose quartz, and turquoise—so much possibility and style.

Of course, I had to question, "Why are you not wearing all these fabulous pieces you own? Look at how much fun you could be having!"

And she said, "Fun? Oh no, this is all overwhelming. When I'm not working, I'm so drained that I can't even process what to do with my clothes. I mean, I love them, but honestly? I'm lazy! Can't style just be easy? I just look at all this stuff and see nothing! What I need is a getting dressed routine that is simple but makes me feel fabulous."

Bingo. *Simple, yet fabulous.* That was exactly what I taught Marissa to do.

"Style *is* easy!" I exclaimed. First, we started with simple tools that anyone can quickly do without thinking. For Marissa, it was teaching her useful style tools that make putting outfits together effortless *and* quick. We worked on building an outfit formula (accessories included) for her that would work each and every time she got dressed.

Remember how I said in the last chapter that your clothes are just clothes, but with accessories, they become an outfit? Let's take Marissa's T-shirt-and-jean-shorts combo, which didn't at all reflect the sassy woman that she was. We updated it by half tucking her T-shirt into her shorts and adding a skinny leopard belt, a rose-quartz pendant necklace, and a pair of tan ankle booties.

What was different here? The detail of the half-tucked shirt helped define her waist. A pop of color in the belt drew attention to her waist as well as adding personality (hello, leopard!) and style to her look. We topped off her basic T-shirt with a knockout statement necklace to give it an intentional detail, and finally, we switched out her sneaks for walkable booties she could rock all day long. It's those small, easy swap-outs and additions that can instantly upgrade an outfit and give something even as plain as a T-shirt and shorts a whole new style and vibe.

Moving forward, Marissa had a recipe for a successful morning experience: add a necklace, add the half-tuck detail, maybe add a belt if she feels so inclined, and choose a shoe option that makes her feel fabulous. And, boom, she's done and out the door with little additional time needed. She looks cool and put together, and even something as simple as her base look—the T-shirt and shorts—is effortlessly stylish.

The thing about style is that it can be learned, and being lazy with your style is 100 percent fixable. As you know, my whole practice is about simple tools. Style should be easy, not overwhelming. It should feel like second nature, not a struggle. Straightforward and applicable tools can literally change your whole style strategy by tomorrow. I am letting you in on all the secrets here. Your style tastes might change, your financial situation may change, your body may change, but these tools? They will never change. You can always refer right to your trusty style survival manual to create effortless style even on the laziest of days. Laissez chic, here you come!

FOUR AND OUT THE DOOR

I developed this technique after years of building outfits for clients. This simple and laissez-chic formula is the instant cure for a no-energy day, an uneventful day, an "I have nothing to wear" day, a "what should I wear" day, an "I have a date tonight" day, an interview day, and just your routine headed-to-the-office day. And yes! This even works if you are just staying at home, running casual errands, or heading to an exercise class. Once you know this style formula, it will never leave you. Instead, it will always be the thing you think about every single time you get dressed no matter what your plan is for the day. Simply ask yourself, *Do I have at least four pieces on today?*

The Four and Out the Door approach to styling is the concept that every outfit you put together should involve a minimum of four noticeable pieces. For each outfit you put on, you should be able to count four or more pieces in your look that support your style. It's important to note that shoes and handbags don't count because, regardless of what you wear, you are always going to put on a pair of shoes and grab your handbag before you walk out the door. So, for now, put those pieces aside and let's start building outfits.

Here's how it works. Each day when you get dressed for work, let's say you put on a blouse and a skirt, or a button-up and a pair of ankle cropped pants. That is just two pieces! It's not until you put on an additional layering piece, like a jacket (in any form) or cardigan, and a piece of jewelry, such as a necklace or a statement earring, that your two pieces of clothing become an outfit. Simple, right?

This formula is not just a simplified way to put outfits together; it also gives you leeway to create your own unique style every day. The options are endless. No matter what your two-piece base is, it's the third and four pieces that will connect the dots of your outfit to your personality and your style messaging. Let's take a classic office look and get creative together.

The Base: a silky printed blouse and solid navy ankle cropped slacks

Keep it professional. Add a tailored or structured blazer and a sparkling statement necklace to frame your face to create your Four and Out the Door. Then add your accessory necessities: a pair of leopard pointed-toe flats and your leather office tote.

Keep it casual. Pop on a denim jacket with the sleeves cuffed and pair with a long pendant necklace. When adding your necessities, continue the casual vibe with a pair of wedge sandals and a pop-of-color crossbody handbag.

Keep it comfortable. Layer on a soft cardigan and lightweight cotton scarf. The perfect necessities here could be your everyday carryall handbag, a wide-brimmed hat, and a pair of white Converse sneaks.

Keep it edgy. Top off your base with a fitted leather motorcycle jacket, styled with a pair of eye-catching earrings. A classic pointed-toe pump and an evening clutch are the perfect partners to continue the style of your look.

This is just one base for you to get creative with using the Four and Out the Door approach. Think about all the other options you can create using different bases, like a T-shirt and jeans, a blouse and skirt, or even a dress. All you have to do is think, *Do I have four pieces on today?* Then, *Do I want to add more?* Because if you are obsessed with accessories and layering like I am, you may want to do so. Add earrings, pop on a belt too, throw on a fun set of bangles you put together, mixing and matching a few different sets. You have the freedom to put on as many pieces as your creative heart desires! Style is all in the details.

This also works on those "athleisure" days. You know the ones I'm talking about—when you find yourself in yoga pants and then opt to stay in them all day. Yes! This tool works here too. If you're committed to wearing yoga pants, at least make it look like you did it on purpose and style an outfit with them. Use Four and Out the Door and make your look effortlessly stylish. Start with your yoga pant and whatever top you may be wearing. Throw on a denim, leather, or motorcycle jacket over your look, and pull it all together with a cool necklace. Throw on some shades, and you are good to go! Nobody will ever know you've had those pants on since the wee hours of the morning. Oh! And don't forget to dry shampoo your 'do, girl!

What makes the Four and Out the Door approach so magical is that it's the fourth piece in your look that tends to be your finishing touch. At its core, it is your ultimate styling tool for accessorizing, because if you only have three pieces on, you most likely don't have an accessory added. Pop on that accessory, you've completed your formula, and then it's up to you what to do next. Add hoop earrings, a few rings, some bangles, a belt, a hat—your whole accessory drawer! I mean, why not? You know what I love to say: Just try it! This is the part of creativity and self-expression that you get to explore more and more each and every day. Watch as your mornings change with this one simple tool.

Instead of feeling that pain of "What am I going to wear today?" you flip that script to "What is going to be my fourth piece for the day?" And you've begun a daily choose-your-own-style adventure game where you get to determine what to do next.

But the best part to this styling trick is that it's timeless. The formula works if your style is classic and simple, rocker and boho (like our friend Marissa), feminine and professional, edgy and sophisticated, or any other creative style name you can come up with for your style. Whatever your style vibe is, this tool works. What has become so clear to me in all my work is that women want style to *be* easy, *feel* easy, and look *effortless*. This will be your number one tool to do that!

WHEN IN DOUBT, BELT IT OUT!

"When in doubt, belt it out" is my favorite and most famous "Laurie-ism." Let this phrase be a reminder to you each and every time you get dressed and you can't put your finger on what is missing. Or when you are looking for that fourth piece! Or when you know you need to show a little more effort in your look than just throwing on clothes. I have been using this philosophy for years. I even have an entire keynote speech about it, entitled "A Great Belt and an Open Mind." True story. This secret styling trick is the one thing you can do tomorrow to change your whole perspective on your style, your body, and yourself. Yep. It's that powerful.

For your style, wearing a belt can change the dynamic of an entire outfit. There are two ways to wear belts: at the high waist, where the smallest part of your frame resides, and at the lower waist, where your belt loops lie. Remember from chapter 6 that defining the waist is the common denominator among all the body shapes. The specific area where your belt is best placed can vary based on the outfit you are wearing. A high-rise jean, for example, may have the belt loops sit around your belly button, while a mid-rise will have your belt loops around your high hip. A dress may have no belt loops at all; same with a pencil skirt or blouse. The challenge is, Can you style a belt into your look when there aren't belt loops to guide you? Pop back over to chapter 4 and find that sweet spot for you.

Wearing a belt adds dimension to your look. The more detail you put into your outfit, the more dimension and visual style it has. Belts also add an opportunity for creativity. Try wearing belts in fun colors or even in a pattern. Leopard, snake, or zebra patterns are great starter prints to play around with. Want a hot styling tip? Animal patterns act as neutrals, so you can wear them with practically anything. Yes, even other prints. By adding a belt to your outfit, you are officially styling with intention. And by adding conscious detail to your look, you instantly enhance your outfit.

Want to know how you wear a belt? Let's refer back to one of my favorite sketches from the IFC show *Portlandia*. It's called "Put a Bird on It!" (If you haven't already seen it, go look it up right now! It's hilarious.) Two bird fanatics go into a store, and they are like "Oh, this handbag looks sad. Put a bird on it!" Or "This shirt needs something more—put a bird on it!" Or "This notebook would look way cuter if you put a bird on it!" When it comes to wearing a belt, I have my own version of this, and it works every time! It's called "Put a belt on it!" Have a flowy blouse? Put a belt on it! Have a block-color dress? Put a belt on it! Have a piece that is too big? *Put a belt on it!* You get the idea. A belt can literally go over anything. You just have to try it.

The funny thing is, countless people have said to me in the course of my career, "Laurie! I don't even own a belt!" Well, if that's you, I recommend you sift through your closet and find that one dress, skirt, or pant that already has a belt that came with it. Or perhaps you can lovingly borrow a belt from your roomie or sister or even out of your partner's closet. I mean, hey! Why not? At least to play around with one and see for yourself. Try throwing it over a blouse, try tossing it over your dress, try it over a pencil skirt with a tucked-in blouse. See what you think. You don't have to commit yet, but it's good to play around and see what is possible for you.

Want to know a wild belt secret? Finding your best belt fit is actually a gateway to empowerment and possibility! For so many women, the idea of adding a belt feels foreign and, frankly, physically uncomfortable. However, whether you wear it over a dress, a skirt, a high-waisted pant, a blouse, a cardigan, or a jacket, a belt at the high waist will accentuate the area of the female form that defines us as women. When we define our waists in this way, we find a new way to look at our female form in the mirror. It can change our perspective on ourselves, our bodies, and our alluring personal appeal.

There are also some seriously empowering benefits here. As women, we don't realize that something as simple as wearing a belt can have a chain reaction in our body, causing us to stand stronger. Wearing a belt forces you to hold your core in, which engages your muscles in creating a longer and leaner presence—and posture! When your core is held in, it then compels you to hold your shoulders back, keep your back straight, and even lift your chin a little. Put your hands on your high waist, Wonder Woman style, and you are ready to take over the world! Hell-o, empowerment pose! We women are strong! Shouldn't we finally wear a wardrobe that makes us feel that way too?

Think back to the mirror moment with Savannah when she finally saw herself in an entirely new, glowing light. The vision of her female body accentuated with a belt reopened her mind to what was possible for her, her body, and her life. Prior to that moment, the feeling of being a powerful woman felt impossible to her, like a distant memory she would never grasp again. Much to her surprise, it was the power of the belt that unlocked a whole new world to her. So, while I can't be there in person to show you in the mirror—*but, girl, would I love to*—I hope this deeper conversation as to why you should consider belting it out takes you on your own self-discovery journey and to your own mirror moment!

When you discover that the "impossible" is actually possible for you, you see how being close-minded can affect how you view what is happening all around you. Think about what else you have said: "Oh, that doesn't work for me," or "I couldn't try that." We've all stopped ourselves. I've done it too! But that mirror moment is when we can break the glass barrier of our minds and allow a light to enter our lives that we could never have imagined. Knowing that, it's time to question, "What else is possible that I may have believed to be impossible for me?" So don't just try the belt for the style, try it for the empowerment and the limitless possibility that it can open up too. Now, that's quite the style tool, isn't it?

THE ART OF TUCKING AND CUFFING

Tucking and cuffing are both incredibly easy and impactful styling tools. Both are really simple updates that you can make to so many outfits that will support balancing your frame and add that look of intentionality while giving even the basics a touch of style. I use these tools daily for myself, and like all the tools in this chapter, it is something you can try the next time you get dressed.

When it comes to tucking, I am referring to "tucking in," which can look different for different people, as well as for different body types. While this will be a very general overview, I hope that you try it for yourself. There are two ways you can tuck: a full tuck and a half tuck. A full tuck is best when you are working with a blouse or top and tucking it into a high-waisted pencil skirt, a full skirt, or a high-waisted pant or jean. By tucking in your top, you are helping define your waist and elongate your leg line and

untucked   *half-tucked*

your frame overall. This helps to enhance the female form by not allowing yourself to hide under a tent of fabric. It also gives you an opportunity to add a belt to further accentuate the area if you so choose.

The half tuck is a personal favorite of mine because it adds a dash of style intention, a dash of body lengthening, and a dash of muffin-top masking. Yup! Muffin-top masking. Here's how you do it: Whether you are wearing something high- or low-waisted, all you have to do is hold the front five to six inches of the hem of the top you are wearing and tuck it into your bottoms. Once tucked in, tug sideways at the edges to loosen the tuck and give it a little drape. Then work your hands around the sides to the back to let the fabric nicely drape over your hips. I love this trick because something as simple as a half-tuck update to a basic blouse-and-jeans combo gives your outfit a stylish, yet effortless, look.

When it comes to cuffing, this is another quick and easy trick you can do with basically any outfit. Cuffing is when you cuff up or flatly fold the hems of either your sleeves or your pants (or both). Let's start with the sleeves. I recommend always cuffing up sleeves, whether it be on a denim jacket, a blazer, a leather jacket, or even a cardigan. A couple of things happen when you cuff up your sleeves. One, it adds another intentional touch to your look. It's something that appears effortless and is subtly effective. Two, when you cuff up your sleeves to show about six to seven inches of your forearm, you are effectively elongating your arms and slimming down your frame visually. Trust me—it works every time. Try it in the mirror! Sometimes when you are wearing certain jackets, fabrics, or color combinations, they feel weighted on the frame. But by cuffing up the sleeve, you lift the look and allow the eyes to continue to make their way up your frame. This is especially helpful if you are petite, like me!

As for your pant hem, here is where you can have a lot of fun, and it works well with boyfriend, slim, or skinny denim. Try cuffing the hem of your denim when wearing heels or ankle booties. Remember when I taught you that horizontal lines can be widening? Well, this is one of those break-the-rule moments. Cuffing your hem will create a horizontal line at your ankle, but when you show the slimmest part of your ankle, it is surprisingly lengthening, especially if you wear a nude-tone, tan, metallic, or warm-colored flat, heel, or bootie. This will also support the continuation of the leg line. Something to remember: this trick will work against you if you try it with flats or even some pumps. But I think pumps can go either way. The idea is that you are adding a very easy to do, additional detail into your outfit that doesn't take a lot of effort but offers a lot of style.

STYLING WITH CONTRASTS

Contrasts are another one of my favorite styling tricks because every time I try to explain the concept to clients they always say, "Wait, what??!! I can do that?" My answer is always, "Yes! Yes, you can!" I really do love debunking people's own personal myths about themselves and their style and creating a whole new space for outfit creation and opportunity. This styling tool is a BIG one for that. There are so many misconceptions about how we should be wearing our clothes: Your casual clothes should be worn casually. Your dressy clothes should be worn when dressing up. Your professional clothes are only meant for the office.

Well, I'm thrilled to break it to you, but these are absolutely fashion rules that you can throw out the window too. You can mix your dressy and your everyday, your casual with your professional, your daytime with your nighttime, your sexy with your basic, your soft with your structured, your flowy with your leather, your feminine with your masculine, your creative with your classic, your feminine with your edgy, and on and on. See what I am getting at? Styling with contrasts offers you endless opportunities to express yourself.

Here are a few classic style concepts you can mix pieces of together and play around with what you may already own!

The casual: jeans, joggers, a T-shirt, sneakers and a neutral skinny belt

The dressy: a structured blazer, a silky blouse, dress or skirt, a statement necklace, and classic pumps

The feminine: a flirty dress, a flowing skirt, soft colored blouses, lace, a pink belt, and colorful tassel earrings

The edgy: a leather motorcycle jacket, lace-up boots, spiked jewelry, and metal details

The classic professional: a tailored skirt or pant suit, a poplin blouse or button down, and a structured handbag

The creative: a printed blouse, a colored jacket, conversational accessories and bright heels

The best part about styling in contrasts is that by incorporating contrasting ideas into your outfit, you are in actuality designing a look that reflects the true you. Women are complicated and multifaceted. We are both sensitive and strong, soft and hard, feminine and edgy. Women are not just one thing, and neither is our style. Our style should be a reflection of all the aspects of who we are. When you learn to mix up all those fabulous aspects of you into your wardrobe, you will have a recipe for dynamic style that not only represents all the areas of you but creates an eye-turning je ne sais quoi!

SHINE IN YOUR SHOES

When it comes to styling, you probably know that shoes are an important part of your look. But did you also know that your shoe has some significant power over your outfit? Yep! Your shoes can dictate your outfit intention for you without you having to do much. This is a styling tool that is really supportive for moms, supermoms, and superwomen all around. You know, that extremely busy, on-the-go, need-to-shift-from-day-to-night-, from-office-to-mom-, or from-work-to-network-in-minutes kind of life? Your shoes are the key.

Here's what you need to know: your shoes determine your outfit's vibe. Let's take a simple flirty dress and denim jacket outfit. Wearing that with a pair of cool sneakers or retro kicks gives the outfit a casual vibe. Style with a pair of gladiator sandals, and you've added in a fashion vibe. Put on a pair of pumps, and you now have a date-night vibe. Wear with a pair of short booties, and you have a dressed-up Saturday vibe. Wear with a tall riding boot and pop on a scarf, and you are pre-fall perfection. The idea is that you can change up your shoe without having to change up your outfit to create a whole new look. Wearing pumps for the office? Switch into booties for dinner with your partner and kids. Wearing sandals during the day? Update with a pair of heels for a last-minute date. Wearing sneakers while running errands? Shift into boots for a Saturday-night outing. You get the idea! Style doesn't have to be complicated or require a lot of thought. Even something as easy as changing your shoe can change your outfit entirely.

PUTTING IT INTO PRACTICE

Style is in the details. It's in how you carry yourself, and it's especially in how you feel about yourself. While the reaction of feeling confident about your style comes with time and consistency, the more you practice, the more you will see how worthy, fabulous, and valuable you are. The details of what you wear are very easily fixable. If you're simple or trendy, professional or totally "extra"—that's all up to you!

I want you to start thinking differently. I mean, that is basically what this whole book is getting at. I want you to think differently not just about your style but also about what is possible for you. Working through these tools will continue to help you home in on what feels great for you. They offer you ample means of creativity and opportunity each time you open the closet door. Not sure where to start? Pick out a fun top before you go to bed, and in the morning, build your outfit around it. Next evening pick a pant or skirt, then build another outfit the morning after. Day after day, you practice a little more. Getting dressed and creating a style all your own will become less overwhelming and more of an exciting part of your morning. You won't just think, *What am I going to wear today?* but instead, *What do I GET to wear today?*

so, let's recap!

- Style is easy when you have tools you can use every day to help you build an outfit that is dynamic, creative, and reflective of you. Those tools will help guide you to living your life with effortless style. Not only will you look effortless, but putting your looks together will feel effortless too! It's Laissez-Chic City from now on!

- The Four and Out the Door system is your everyday go-to style tool that will force you to ask yourself every morning, Do I have four pieces on today? Do you?

- When in doubt, belt it out! It's a simple phrase to help you remember that adding a belt is not just for the style but for your empowerment too. Trust me; it works every time!

- Cuff and tuck your look. Sometimes, it is the smallest of details you can incorporate into your look that will have the biggest impact on your style! Let cuffing and tucking be those quick details to add that will support your style swagger in a simple fold.

- Style with contrast. Incorporate all the different and beautiful aspects of you and your life into your look by using the tool of styling with contrasts. That way, you can show off your best you every time you get dressed.

- Shine in your shoes. Your shoe choice can easily update your outfit and your style direction. No matter what you are wearing, opt for a shoe that suits your mood, your vibe, or your message. This is a big part of your style; it's your decision. You pick your expression!

style statement

I see possibility every time I get dressed. Style is easy! Style is fun! Most importantly, my style is all up to me. By using the tools of style, I am letting the world know who I am.

PART IV

shining from the
inside out

CHAPTER 9

dressing with intention

SHIFTING YOUR STYLE PERSPECTIVE

Your image is such an important and valuable part of your style and your life. It's your personal style strategy that you get to make your own. It is what speaks for you, what sells for you, and what tells a story about you. And you get to design that story however you choose. I mean, that's why we're here, right? To create a new mindset of what is possible for you and your style. The style that reflects your best *you*, the style that shares your incomparable *you*, the style that exclaims to the world who *you* are and what *you* stand for.

Take a moment to think about this: Does your current wardrobe reflect the most confident, powerful, smart, savvy, dynamic, energetic, forward-thinking, and empowered you? If your response is no, you are NOT alone. The truth is, most people struggle with feeling personally empowered. And I know from personal experience that it can feel easier to just stay stuck, overwhelmed, too busy, uninspired, or all of the above than to pull yourself together in order to shine.

As women, we evolve. We grow, we gain experience, we move up to the next level, we start our own businesses, we meet the one, we get married, we have children, our bodies change, our skin changes, our hair even changes. Whatever our life paths may be, we change over and over and over again. But here's what happens: As our lives evolve and we continue to grow, we start to prioritize everyone and everything else above ourselves. The kids need dinner. A deadline forced you to miss a friend's birthday. You find less and less time for self-care. You wear the same things over and over again. When we put ourselves last, we can very often forget to take care of the most important thing in our lives: OURSELVES!

This is one of the biggest reasons why I am hired by my clients. With all this evolution happening around us, and because of our dedication and devotion to our work, our lives, and our families, we lose sight of one very important detail that can change everything. We lose sight of ourselves and, in turn, our style. And losing our sense of style is, in actuality, an act of losing that deep inner connection to the special beings that we are.

But when we become the last priority in our own lives, it shows in our wardrobe, in our outfit choices, and, yes, in our energy field. Years can go by, stuck in a bad style routine, with a dated wardrobe, wearing the same outfits, and never feeling like we have time to get anything new. This is not a positive way to experience clothes. And that negative self-talk that can happen is a detriment to how you experience your whole self, your clothes, and your style. That is how we so easily fall into our bad style patterns. Style is a way to empower yourself during tough times, sad days, and insecure moments. Style shares a powerful message about who you are to the world around you. Your style can lift you up and make you smile, make others smile, spark a conversation, and create bonds.

And don't think for a moment that just because I'm a stylist I am immune to this. I've totally been there! Many times, actually, but most recently when I became a mother. The first year of motherhood, I experienced this challenge in a whole new light. For months straight, my style uniform was a pair of sweat pants, a function-over-fashion nursing bra, and an oversized sweatshirt—the utter antithesis of who I am! Wearing that every day for weeks at a time pushed me further and further away from myself, my wardrobe, and my empowered sense of style. I would longingly look at my closet and start thinking to myself, *I used to be fun!* or *I used to be such a warrior!* or *These clothes used to fit!* or *I used to feel so good in my skin!* or *I used to feel like a woman!*

Been there too? Whether it's from new motherhood, or when you finally come up for air in the busy day-to-day hamster-wheel life we can all feel caught in, it's so common. And great news! You still are that same amazing woman you remember so fondly. She's still in there! Just as I have powered through, here's something to keep you looking forward too. A reminder that when we change our perspective about what we see, a whole world of possibility opens up to us. Remember this always: The "old you" does not determine the future you. The you yesterday doesn't determine the future you, for that matter, either. The present you does. The you right now. The you that will walk to her closet doors tomorrow and say, "What am I going to wear today?" Which means that each day you get to start anew and style yourself to be whoever and whatever you want to be. Bring that kind of intention to your closet and unlock the superpower of style.

STYLE IS YOUR VISUAL BUSINESS CARD

Consider this: *style* is your visual business card. Yes, your style speaks for you before you say a word. It is 100 percent what people see first when you walk into a room. It is what people will consider before they even hear your pitch. It is what people will judge you on before they even know you. Simply put, your style tells a story—your story. The story behind your wardrobe. But! When you take control of your wardrobe, your personal style can be the messenger of the story you WANT to share.

That's some powerful stuff right there. I experienced it firsthand at the beginning of my career, yet I have learned to master it as I have grown in my professional life. I always made it a priority for my wardrobe to not only speak for me but to also start the conversation. I learned this technique while working in New York City as a fashion designer. While the fashion industry may have been tough, nothing made me feel better than getting a compliment on my outfit or even meeting somebody new on account of a unique piece I was wearing. In my almost twenty-year career, connections, conversations, and friendships happened over a pair of green shoes, a silk scarf tied around a handbag, even the eye-catching mixed-print dress in a sea of black, or a sparkling oversized statement necklace. That's just some of the magic hidden in style.

My personal style and sense of creativity became the perfect tools for me as I built my career from scratch, built my business from nothing, and navigated the ups and downs of entrepreneurship. Things may have always been changing, but one thing remained: my style was and is always a representation of the woman I am. My brand is my image and my image is my brand. Your image is your brand too. And when it comes to business your personal expertise, unique interest, and dynamic quality are your products to sell. What you wear is the catchy tagline and visual message about your product. We've all walked through our favorite retailer when something catches our eye, excites us, and maybe even lands in our cart. That packaging! You love the color palette, the typography is so cool, the product overall is different. Sold! For the record, there's absolutely no shame in judging a product's quality and usefulness and then buying it based on its packaging. I have been known to purchase a bottle of wine because it was metallic and shaped like a cat! Was the wine good? Not so much, but I kept the bottle as décor! However, when it comes to people, I don't recommend judging and instead approach this as assessing. That way, you can look at style, color, details, and expression as something to analyze creatively as well as to give you subtle clues about the wearer. Because just as you gravitated toward the unique packaging of the product on the shelf, the same goes for how we gravitate toward people and, more importantly, how people gravitate toward us. **Our clothing is our packaging, and our style is our message to the world.**

Remember that I told you that your *image* was a secret superpower? Well, here's where things become interesting. You have the ability to strategize your wardrobe to make the most of any situation you are in. But before we get into the specifics, it's important to know some bigger strategies that are your base ingredients to your own personal style elixir.

First and foremost, always, is *fit*. We discussed the truth about fit, but let's peel another layer deeper. Fit has changed drastically over the last twenty years. However, I can attest from my professional clients that while the times change, more often than not, we overlook updating our suits, jackets, and professional wear to fit the new modern vibe. Instead, we continue to wear those pieces that are dated, faded, or ill-fitting. *Hey, don't worry, you are not alone!* That means it is time to invest in new and modern fitted pieces that will flatter your figure and look sharp on your frame. The slimmest line will always be the most flattering (in other words, go get a tailor). And don't forget, waist definition is a must!

Historically speaking, for men or women to have properly tailored suits or dresses meant that they had to come from prestige, power, and money. Today, while style is much more expansive than that, the impression still remains and can be used to your advantage. Wearing clothes that fit you properly will give you that more expensive, more modern, and more prestigious look. This styling strategy works for women of all ages. For a young professional, it can help you appear more mature and credible, and for a more seasoned professional, the proper fit can make you appear fresh and contemporary. But my favorite part about what fit says about us as women? It shows a total awareness of and an outright body-love confidence with the skin you are in.

One of the easiest, quickest, and most effective updates you can make to your wardrobe to shift your visual impression and the message you send is to invest in a tailored-to-you blazer. I'm talking about one that sits right at your shoulders with no additional shoulder padding, tapers in at the waistline with tailored dart details, and has a clearly defined waist with only one or two buttons max. This kind of jacket will instantly elevate your overall professional look without you having to try too hard. Trust me, when you put that properly fitted blazer on, you will see an instantaneous result. You'll look like a million bucks and, more importantly, you will *feel* that way too. The good news is that you don't have to spend a fortune to look that way! Be open to exploring different price points and brands and various tailored fits until you find the right one for you. And when all else fails, have a close-to-perfect jacket tailored. It will be worth every penny!

Paying attention to details is another important factor to the impression you make. Are the heels of your shoes scuffed? Is there a tear in your leather handbag strap? Is there a missing button you are hoping nobody notices? It's the little things that can diminish the value of a look. Attention to those details shows that you are conscientious about yourself. How does this read to others? Somebody who is thoughtfully aware of their personal presentation, even down to the smallest detail, may also be very detail oriented in their work, which is a powerful quality to show. Does that mean you need to be the picture of perfection every time you put yourself together? Not at all! We are all imperfect, and there is always space and grace for those days when it doesn't all come together. The magic is in your overall consistency. Nail it most of the time, and you are still winning.

Which leads perfectly to my next point: having a consistent signature is another style strategy you can work with at any time, in business and life. Well, actually every time you step out the door. The idea is to have something that you always do consistently. Is it that you always have a bold colored tassel earring? Is it that you always wear interesting shoes? Is it a necklace? How you tie your scarf around your handbag? Or how you are always wearing something with leather? Or stripes? Or outfitted in all-out color? (Or even all black for those who love black!) It's something for people to remember you by, and being memorable is another magic spell that will continue to reveal itself over and over again.

Lastly, and most importantly, the key to your magnetic visual business card is *confidence*. It is composed of self-ownership, embodiment, self-love and acknowledgement (which ultimately this book is here to support you in doing). Confidence will always be your best accessory and eye-catching visual enhancer no matter what outfit you put on. If you feel great in what you are wearing, you will look great. Not only will people notice, they will walk right up to you and introduce themselves too. It's the Law of Attraction at its best. Your vibrational energy when you feel confident blasts out signals far beyond what your wardrobe can. It's the ultimate device in magnetizing the magic you are creating in your life with your style.

SHOWING UP AS YOUR BEST YOU

Let's talk about everyday intention in your wardrobe. I bet you have that one dress or outfit you hold on to for those "special occasions." Maybe it's the one you wear to a big meeting or an interview, or maybe it's the one you save for a memorable date night. It fits you well, you feel fabulous in it, and when you wear it you shine with confidence. Those are the best kind of outfits, no? But it's so funny because we all have that outfit or item in our closet, yet we hold on to it for that perfect moment when it is ready to be removed from the depths of your closet and be worn for a single day or night out in your life.

It's always been my philosophy that we should put more intention into mornings by actively choosing to wear clothes that make us feel fantastic, every single day. So why is it we tend to save our best looks for a particularly special moment? Shouldn't every day be considered special? I sure think so! And if that is the case, that means that every single day should get a special outfit. It should be something you love that fits your mood, your day ahead, and, most importantly, makes you shine! It's okay if you don't have any meetings scheduled for the day and the only person who is going to see you is your lovingly devoted dog. It's also okay if you're just sitting at your desk all day. Intentionally dressing in a power outfit helps you recognize that not only every day is special but you are special too.

When you wear something that makes you feel good, the feeling infuses everything around you! You can't be in a bad mood when you feel like a badass! Wearing something that steps up your style game on the daily will actually help you take yourself and your work more seriously. Have you ever noticed your productivity level on the days you are dressed more confidently? There is most definitely a correlation between what you wear, how you feel, and how you execute your work. One of my favorite reasons to wear your best every day is because people notice. They take you seriously, they treat you differently, they see you differently because you see yourself for who you are and you are showing up as your best you.

So let's start identifying those power outfits going forward. Give yourself a little self-care "me time" to complete this small task to help you on your way to everyday empowerment. First, pull from your closet all those power pieces—jackets, dresses, tops, bottoms, accessories, shoes, and anything else that applies. With those pieces, build out seven to ten days' worth of outfits that fit your lifestyle and schedule, in the style that makes you feel like your best you. Don't be afraid to take risks too! Have fun with it. Next, wear them! Choose a different outfit each day and challenge yourself to commit! Take a picture of each look you wear and start a photo file. This will be your personal style file to help you remember awesome outfits, inspire you to create more, and keep you organized and in check with your wardrobe. As you continue to build new outfits that you love over time, keep your style diary handy so you can reference them, expand from them, and even be inspired to create new outfits going forward. This style tool is so valuable because on those days when you don't have as much time and are rushed through your morning practice, you now have a style support system to guide you. You can use one of your previous outfits as a jumping-off point, or just wear it head to toe. It's entirely up to you!

The idea is that we want getting dressed to be easy but also intentional!

And just like everything else, the more you do it, the easier it becomes. Yes, you have to go through those uncomfortable days when you feel like you are *way* overdressed for your office to get more comfortable dressing that way. Even if your coworker makes a snarky comment like "Have an interview today, do we?" Or perhaps somebody says, "Who are *you* dressing up for?" Your answer? "Me! I'm dressing up for me! And I love it." Those types of comments should never stop you from dressing your most stunning *you*. Style is a choice, and when you push through those uncomfortable moments, your daily style practice will become your new normal along with a newly empowered style mindset.

SUBLIMINAL STYLE MESSAGING

Let's go another layer deeper. Would you believe that within our style choices subliminal messages are being put off? Sounds creepy, but the visual impression behind different details, such as accessories, shapes, silhouettes, fabrics, and colors, actually tells more story than we realize. But! Here's the cool part: knowing what those cues are gives you the opportunity to fine-tune as well as amplify your message. Using this unspoken aspect of style, you can tailor (pun intended) your style to fit your day-to-day needs, wants, and desires. You can play up or play down certain qualities. You can enhance or distract from different features. You can even influence the perception of others. When styling with this intention tool, it's all about using your image to communicate your specific and unique message.

Playing with perception definitely has an ominous ring to it, but in actuality it's a very positive tool that you can play with to help you step into who you are. It's a way to think even a little deeper about what you are wearing and what it says about you. That's true intentionality! More intention behind your look means you are getting dressed consciously. You really have to think, *Who am I, and how do I shine as my best me?* The answer may be different from day to day, but that consciousness and daily acknowledgment is exactly what helps you rise up to be your best you. Because when you dress the way you want to be, it can help empower you to not only feel it, but to begin to see it and eventually to believe it. Remember, YOU are already "it." You ARE the style!

Let's play with some magic potions to help you go even deeper with how to share who you truly are, through your wardrobe. Here are the main concepts to play with in your own personal style. Always start with asking yourself, *Who am I, and how do I want people to perceive me today?* Play all the various aspects of you that you want to share, up or down, as you please. This is the "science" (more like the magic) of dressing with detailed intention to create a more empowered you.

Very generally speaking, straight and angular lines, high-contrast color combinations, and structured garments and fabrics all exhibit the qualities of strength, authority, power, edge, and girlbossness. *Is that even a word?!* Conversely, curved lines, low-contrast color combinations, and soft garment construction and fabrication all express approachability, softness, femininity, and friendliness. It's these opposing sides of our personality that can be portrayed through our wardrobe. The fun part—and this is where the magic happens—is when you learn to play up or play down any given concept in order to send off your compelling messages. Walking into a meeting and want to feel powerful yet approachable? Styling a structured blazer and tailored pant or pencil skirt mixed with a soft silk low-contrast printed blouse helps you hit both of those messages in your wardrobe. A rounded-toe shoe will continue to add a friendlier approach, while a pointed-toe shoe will add a little more control and edge. See what I mean? Let's break down each concept further so you can start playing around and brewing up more magic tricks in your life and wardrobe.

LINES VS. CURVES

In all our faces we have lines and angles, and we also have curves. Some have more dominant lines and angles than others. This translates into sharp pointed eyebrows, straight eyes, an angular nose, and lip points by your Cupid's bow (you know, that cute little divot under your nose). Angles can look like a sharper jawline or a very square and angled face. Women that have more lines and angles in their facial structure can seem unapproachable, edgy, superior, and unsociable. Curves can look like arching eyebrows, almond or round eyes, fuller noses, and softer lips. You can catch curves in a smiling round cheek bone, and you can see roundness in the facial structure too. Women who have more curves and fuller or round faces can seem softer, sweeter, approachable, and friendly.

The idea with designing your message is that you can play up or play down your angles and your curves by using your wardrobe to enhance your facial features. Clothing with lots of angles and edges will pull out the lines in your features and enhance your strength and edge. On the other hand, clothing with a softness and/or rounded edging or details will pull out the curves and enhance your approachability. A few simple examples would be the difference between a classic pointed collar on a button-up shirt versus a rounded Peter Pan collar, or a V-neck shirt versus a scoop-neck shirt. A blazer with sharp edges on its lapel will look stronger, while a cardigan with a shawl collar will appear gentle.

Your hairstyle also plays a part in this. Wear your hair wavy or curly and you will play up your curves and softness. Wear your hair straight, or center parted and pulled back, and you will play up your angles. With all this knowledge you can play up or play down your angles and curves to match your intentions for your next professional outing. You can even use this for dating!

HIGH-CONTRAST COLOR VS. LOW-CONTRAST COLOR

When it comes to color, there is a very simple concept of color theory you can use to support your visual messaging. A high-contrast color combination is when dark or bold saturated colors are paired with white or ivory. Black and white, red and white, brown and ivory, navy and white, charcoal gray and ivory, cobalt blue and white, or burgundy and ivory, for example. Wearing these color combinations together, either in your clothing or even in a print, adds authority and strength and is more commanding visually.

Low-contrasting colors are combinations that look closer in color level. Examples of low-contrast color combinations are black and tan, light gray and white, brown and peach, navy and lavender, and olive and pink. There are a ton of variations in here that create a lower-contrasting look. Low contrast can appear softer, approachable, and kind. The idea here is that, depending on where you are going and what you will be doing, you can use your color contrast to support your messaging. Prints should also be considered. High-contrast prints with sharp-edged patterns will have a stronger look, while painterly floral patterns in low-contrast combinations will feel more romantic and sweeter.

Let's say you're walking into a meeting to sell your client on your absolutely ground-breaking product or service. You're wearing a black blazer, a crisp white button-up shirt, dark skinny jeans, and nude pointed-toe pumps. High-contrasting colors as well as sharp angles and lines will enhance your visual message: "I know what I am doing, and I am going to deliver for you." Or conversely you want to come off as relatable, down to earth, and accessible. You may style a peach scoop-neck, soft floral dress (with waist definition of course), a camel draped-fit blazer, and a tan ankle boot. This says, "I'm put together, but I'm friendly and creative." These are two extremes, but imagine the possibility of playing up or playing down the various aspects of the story you want to share. It is these incredible little cues we can add into our wardrobe mix that begin to sing our own melody.

STRUCTURE VS. SOFTNESS

Continuing with the theme of hard versus soft: *Structure* refers to garments that literally have structure built into their shape or material. For example, a blazer, a pair of slacks, a pencil skirt, and a sheath dress—fabrics that are taut, heavy, sturdy, firm, and crisp. *Softness* refers to garments that have fluidity, ease, and movement to them, such as a silky blouse, a full skirt, a flowing dress, a caftan, or a duster sweater. These fabrics are lightweight, flowing, soft, and draped.

By utilizing strategic shapes and silhouettes, you can continue to play up or play down the messaging and features you want to share. For a stronger, authoritative, and commanding look, wear garments with structure in more taut fabrics. For a softer, approachable, and friendlier look, wear garments that have ease in more relaxed fabrics. Here's a curveball for you! What about a garment built with structure but in a fabric with ease? Like a structured blazer but in a double-knit fabric? Well, then you have found the perfect blend of mastering the message of strength and softness in a single item.

There are literally thousands of combinations you can create when mixing and matching elements of strength and softness into your look. As a rule of thumb, in any face-to-face business transaction (when you get dressed to represent your best self), there should always be elements of your strength *and* your softness. I mean, we are women! That is our ultimate power!

There is only one disclaimer here because, while I can't be in every closet, I want to empower you with something to help you as you navigate this in our own life. Always trust your gut. If it feels off, it most likely *is* off. But don't let that discourage you! There is so much possibility, and the more you create, take for test drives, tweak, and re-create, the stronger your message will become.

Styling and presenting yourself this way will create a more dimensional perception of who you are and the style story you want to tell about yourself. Every time you get dressed you have to consider what you are wearing for the day that will support your mood, your message, and your personal mission. You can use your wardrobe to tell the whole picture of you. Whether you play around with some of the guides here or all of them, getting dressed should feel more conscious, present, and intentional. Don't just wear clothes to cover your body, wear clothes to show the world who you really are!

so, let's recap!

- Evolve! Times may have changed, but don't give up on your style or yourself. Create a new mindset of what is possible for you and your style. Your style conveys the story of the incomparable you. Let your style expression exclaim to the world, "I have arrived!"

- Style is your visual business card. Your style tells a story—your story and the story behind your wardrobe. Take control of your wardrobe, put more intention behind it, show up as your best you, and your personal style can be the messenger of the story you WANT to share.

- Don't save your clothes for a special occasion. Every day is special because you are special. Now is the time to put more intention into your mornings by actively choosing to wear clothes that make you feel fantastic, every single day. Identify those power pieces in your closet and get dressed.

- Styling yourself with intention is a powerful tool to play with in your wardrobe. By using more subliminal style cues, you can amplify your unique message. Remember, a powerful woman is both strong and soft. You can dress to be both and share the story of the multifaceted you.

style statement

I honor the incredible being that I am by being intentional when I get dressed so that the story

I share with the world is one that I write.

CHAPTER 10

together we rise

MY SPIRITUAL STYLE AWAKENING

When I was living in the fast-paced world of New York City in the 2000s, I studied Kabbalah. (More spiritual stuff! But just you wait, it's going to tie right back into style with a neat little empowering bow.) I love learning about connecting to the higher power in a spiritual way and then connecting that back to our everyday lives on the ground. And at the time, I needed it! Working in the New York City fashion industry was all consuming, mind, body, and soul. Kabbalah as a whole is a lot to explain, but it is simply a form of spirituality that teaches you to live your most powerful and energetic life by connecting with the Source, the light, energy, God—whatever you would like to call it.

We learn that happiness, joy, and love—the feelings that most people search for in life—are not tangible things and can't be fulfilled by something physical or material. Instead, they are intangible. *Like style!* We learn that those powerful energies are something we cannot fulfill with physical items or material possessions, but rather, through acts of selflessness, we can tap into the powerful, life-fulfilling energies behind the material curtain, so to speak.

As I studied, expanded my thinking, and explored the world with an opened mindset, a few concepts really stuck out to me. The first was the topic of *karma*. Every action has a reaction—positive or negative. Like a seed planted at one point in time that reverberates its effects from that point forward. With Eastern-religion-based roots, karma is a concept widely understood in the Western world. I mean, who hasn't seen a bad driver cut them off and then thought, *He's got some baaaad karma coming his way.* I'm even guilty of thinking that about people I know: a friend who hurt me, a boyfriend who cheated me, a coworker who betrayed me. *Boy, do they have some bad karma piled up!* Oh, and that sweet schadenfreude and the possibility of seeing that karma come to life. But that's all negative karma. What about positive karma? When you help an elderly woman across the road, or give extra time to a friend who needs a shoulder to cry on, or maybe donate your time with a volunteer organization that you care about, those acts of kindness karmically matter too!

This leads me to the second concept that really struck a chord with me: performing acts of selflessness. In a world of "me, me, me," by being selfless, you are not only resisting your own personal self-centered tendencies, but you are also creating powerful positive energy in your life. *Oh, hi again, Law of Attraction.* Overall, this is a very, very simplistic way to explain a few concepts in the complex teachings of Kabbalah, and there is so much more that can be covered, but for the purposes of my Stylepowerment epiphany that I had during this time in my life, I think this is a good start for you.

When I was studying Kabbalah, I was smack in the throes of the New York City fashion industry. Day to day, I was using the art of my style to empower and elevate my mood and energy. Yet on the inside I was on a constant search for deeper meaning as I faced some of the hardest years of my life.

Every time I ventured to work, I could always feel eyes on me; I could feel their stares. Why are they looking at me? Are they judging me? Do I look ridiculous? Should I be embarrassed about something? My head was full of negative thoughts running rampant. Regardless of how that triggered some of my deepest insecurities, I would try to smile and keep my chin held high. What else was I supposed to do?

And those peering eyes went both ways; I too was always looking at other people's outfits. And more negative thoughts would enter my mind. Seeing somebody else in a fantastic outfit can trigger negative feelings about them or ourselves. We quietly muster in our mind, *Oh, well, I could never wear that*, or *She is sooo cute in that. I'm not that cute at all.* We let the feeling of insecurity creep into our being. Or *Ewe, she's so skinny. I'll never look like that*, sending judging negativity her way and back toward yourself. Or ever said this one? "I could never afford that; I'll always be broke." Such subtle but negative thinking! But you most definitely are not alone, we've all been there. Instead of feeling positive or empowered, we stir up insecurities, personal pains, and negative thought patterns. We sometimes even question our worth.

Then one day in Kabbalah class we learned all about the evil eye. What it is, how to stop that energy from entering our space, and how to break the cycle of darting it off to other people, consciously or not. The concept of the evil eye, which is seen in many different cultures, is to, by a glance, send malicious and negatively charged thoughts in another person's direction. And it struck me: Have I been doing this all my life? While yes, I loved to look at other people's outfits, more often than not thinking their outfit was cool, I was simultaneously thinking something negative about the person or myself. It is so easy to do that! So here I was, sitting in class, thinking, *Uh-oh. I've been shooting off the evil eye, left and right, morning and night! This can't be good.*

I became so conscientious of my thoughts from that day forward. I could see how easy it was to let that negative self-view take control in my mind, triggering me to fall deeper into my own perceived insecurities. I began to use the tools I had learned to shift my perspective, and it entirely changed the world around me. Here's the secret: the quick remedy to reverse the evil eye is to very intentionally think positive thoughts in place of negative thoughts. For example, instead of looking at another girl's skirt and defaulting to a judgmental, negative thought about her or yourself, say to yourself, *Wow! That skirt is so beautiful! I wish her ten more beautiful skirts!* and carry on with your day. Groundbreaking, right? Not only do you think something positive, but you send a wish for more beauty and abundance into their life. It's that act of selflessness and resistance to the negativity that creates a powerfully positive energy that can continue to envelop you and permeate into your life. Which is also—karma. The good kind.

I took this newfound and empowering knowledge and hit the streets with it. I wondered what magic I could create by intentionally sending out positive vibes to the strangers I passed on the street. The first few girls I passed, I did exactly as I was told. I caught myself after observing something in their outfit that I loved, and before I could say, feel, or think something negative, I would pause and think instead, *I wish her ten more of those fabulous outfits*, or whatever I was focusing on. It was actually quite uplifting! Over time, I started to make more eye contact with anyone whose outfit tickled my style fancy, or something that wasn't even my style but was so cool or put together! I would catch their eye and smile to them. That also felt really good. And I know that smiling is infectious. While my work life at the time wasn't necessarily the positive experience I wanted in my career, at least when I was walking to and from work, I was putting out a positive vibe with every step and every stylish outfit I passed.

Until one day I passed a girl who was wearing an outfit that was so fabulous, it took my breath away, and instead of just smiling and thinking positively about her and something positive for myself, I blurted out, "Omigod! I *love* your outfit!"

She looked up at me and smiled so big and said with such gratitude, "Thank you!"

We both carried on with our morning walk. Wow, I felt great! I carried that good feeling with me the rest of the day. All I did was compliment her, but it was so fun to surprise her with a completely unexpected compliment. It hit me. *I think I just made her morning. And I made my morning too! What an amazing feeling for us both!* When I arrived at work, which typically felt like a drag, I had a smile on my face, a bounce in my step, and even a little fire inside, kicking my productivity up a notch.

Then, to my utter surprise, my boss approached me and said, "Wow, Laurie! Great blouse today!"

I was in shock! A compliment from my boss? He never noticed me.

My big epiphany came crashing into my soul like a jolt of lightning. *Wait . . . if I give a compliment, will I receive a compliment? Did that small act of selflessness create my own personal positive karmic impact?* What a revelation. I tried it again and again. What I discovered was astonishing. In every instance I genuinely complimented a stranger about their outfit, or a piece they were wearing, or the jewelry they had on, I always received an unsolicited compliment in my own life! I was on to something, and it was big.

THE KARMA CLAUSE

This powerful awakening led me to create what I call the Karma Clause of style—something you may not think about regularly but when you start to incorporate it into your life, it can be absolutely day changing as well as style enhancing. It's my goal that you start using this tool immediately in your life. What I discovered in my years of utilizing this approach to style is, not only is there an energetic cause and effect, there is a physical one as well, and they go hand in hand. When you see somebody wearing an outfit or an item you like and you compliment them out of the blue, it makes their day a little brighter, but it also adds a confident bounce to their step! When they start feeling more confident in their look, they start to stand taller, walk stronger, and even smile! Their energy begins to radiate! By complimenting somebody, you are allowing and even giving them the permission to glow!

Here's the converse reaction: when you compliment someone, it makes you feel good too. You did a selfless act. You sent a positive vibe in someone else's direction that uplifted them, which is uplifting to you too! What happens when you feel good and uplifted? You stand up straighter, you walk stronger, and you smile! It's the same physical reaction from the compliment on both sides. Energetically, the karma finds its way back to you and to others. Your complimented stranger may feel so inclined to compliment somebody else, acknowledging how great that made her feel and wanting to pay it forward. And for you? That compliment will make its way back to you too. Maybe that day, maybe within minutes, maybe the next day. Regardless, watch as you continue to spread positive energy through a simple selfless act of genuinely complimenting and thus empowering other women you see while creating positive energy for yourself at the same time. Cool, right?

Let's walk through the steps together because, while they are simple, I feel there is a strategy and an overall awareness that matters in making the magic. The first step is to be openhearted. Having an open heart and an open mind will reveal a new world around you. When you are open, you see things differently, you spot more opportunities for positivity, and your eyes become more aware of aspects of your surroundings that delight you. Focusing on the positive with a positive frame of mind can help you see more positivity in the world around you.

Conversely, we all know what happens when we are in a negative mood or a bad place—that's all we can see! Positivity is the same way. Having an openness to the world, an openness in your mind, and an openness in your heart will bring to light the intricate beauties of the world and allow you to take them into your soul.

Next is to drop that comparison game. Love thy neighbor. See the beauty in everyone and everything around you. Even in the things you don't like. We are all *sooo* different, and we are all beautiful in our own ways. As women, that is something that should not only be acknowledged but celebrated! Another bright light should not dim your own. Trust me, this is something I've been working on for years with myself. The comparison game can really take its toll on how we view ourselves and the world around us. When we let that mentality win, we are taking away an opportunity to be our best selves. One woman's success and story does not diminish your own. Same goes for style; one woman's style is her style, and by no means does that diminish the light or the value of your own style. It's our own mental mind game we repeatedly play with ourselves that diminishes us, not the woman who triggered it.

Another piece to the puzzle is to be genuine. This has been a cardinal rule for me throughout this process. It doesn't serve you to just throw empty and meaningless compliments to people in order to have compliments find their way back to you. This only works if you are genuine about what excites you. Is it a color? A print? A shoe? A whole look? A vibe? Go with what your gut tells you. Offer your compliment to someone when you truly love what you see. Because it's not just the words you say, it's how you express your words that carries the invisible energy transfer. It is that authentic vibration that transcends the words, and the compliment then plants the seeds for your karma and positive energy to bloom around you. Bottom line: dish them when you mean them.

Lastly, do it as often or as little as you feel it. You can be judicious about when and where to give compliments. You can also be strategic about it. If you recall, one of my dearest friends is somebody whom I met because she complimented me, and I genuinely returned that same kind of love with a compliment as well. The same thing happened again with another one of my now best friends. We were both at this big networking event. It was busy, crowded, loud, and overwhelming. We both were relatively new entrepreneurs, making our way networking through the event, until we passed each other and she saw my handbag with a scarf tied around the handle.

Having never seen somebody do that before, she stopped me in my tracks and was like "I LOVE the scarf tied to your handbag! It's *sooo* cool!"

I said with such delight, "Thank you so much! Hi, I'm Laurie."

The rest is history: mutual clients, dear, dear friends, and forever-connected and always-supportive badass girl-bosses! So complimenting others not only plants seeds of karma for you to collect when the time is right, but it also is a gateway to connecting to others! We often attract people of likeness to us, and you never know whom you may connect or collide with in your life. The opportunity would just pass you by if you didn't speak up and say something. Makes you want to keep those eyes open, huh?

Want to know a fun little secret too? This also works for connecting with men.

The Karma Clause can be a mood lifter and an energy infuser in your life. It's an approach you can use every single day if you like, or whenever the mood strikes. It's your personal power tool to pull out of your now bedazzled, but still invisible, tool belt of ways to empower yourself and others. At the core, the Karma Clause is meant to make you feel good by making others feel good.

KINDNESS IS QUEEN

The concept of kindness has always been at the forefront of my work. I care so deeply about my clients and always communicate to them that "this is a nonjudgment space" for them to share with me their style and story. That art of nonjudgment and kindness is so needed in our world. To care about others and to refrain from judging people based on our own perceptions of the world and ourselves. I think this is of vital importance for women. We may all be so different, but the truth is, we are all the same. We all have our challenges, our hardships, our insecurities, and our unique and individual stories that shape who we are. We've all experienced both laughter and tears, happiness and sadness, joy and fear. When passing strangers on the street, you have absolutely no idea what they've been through to be where they are. And yet, it feels so easy to judge people, almost as if it's

something we learned growing up as gossiping girls. We judged people before we even knew or understood them, and in many instances found ways to inflame our own insecurities at the same time.

The Karma Clause is not just an open-hearted way to approach the world around you, but it is also a continuing practice in nonjudgment of and kindness toward others. Being able to see the beauty in everyone, that's the way we can make this world a better place. A place with more heart, more connection, and more love. We are all just humans, and we have a whole range of experiences, good and bad, that define our individual lives. Understanding that notion for every woman you pass will make your thoughts more intentional and more compassionate. The compassion you can cultivate in your soul will lead you to see more possibility, more opportunity, and more connection in the world around you. Be open. Be a bright light. Set that example of kindness and nonjudgment. Kindness is queen! The more you lead the way, the more others will be inspired to lead in their own lives. The Karma Clause: it's your magic trick to spread positivity, empowerment, confidence, and love.

I wholeheartedly believe that, together as women, we can make this world a better place, and for so many, that feeling can be overwhelming as there is so much that needs to be done to accomplish that. On our streets, in our cities, in our government. If you are like me, that overwhelming feeling, instead of fueling you, can make you feel stunned in your place. The Karma Clause is a small, easy, doable task that you can incorporate into your day-to-day life that makes a difference, even in the smallest of ways. I believe we will see change, not from the top down, but from the bottom up. It's the grassroots efforts that are making a difference in our individual communities and in our lives. It's the people doing good on the ground level that creates the true shockwave effects in our society.

The Karma Clause can be your shockwave. While it feels like a small something, the collective expansion of its energetic flow will continue to grow and spread throughout society. That effect can start with you. The example you set will inspire others. You can make a difference, even by doing something as seemingly inconsequential as complimenting a stranger. The power of style is not to be brushed off as something superficial. Instead, it is something that can lead to significant and powerful energy changes. Uplift yourself by uplifting others and you can let your bright light shine in this world, lighting the way for others to do the same.

SETTING THE EXAMPLE AND LEADING THE WAY

When I think back to the beginning of this discovery, I considered, *Why did I just assume that other people were instantly thinking negatively about me when they looked my way?* What if, instead, they were absolutely loving my outfit but didn't know how to express it? Perhaps, while their mind was thinking something positive, their face was telling a different story. Or more so than that, what I realized was that my already negative train of thinking toward myself was causing me to perceive that these women I passed by were also thinking something negative. Oh, how our minds play tricks on us!

I retrained my thinking. Along with the powerful feeling of removing my evil eye, physically and mentally, and replacing it with compliments and positive thoughts, I started to see a change in my perspective. When I caught a pair of eyes looking at me, I didn't just assume something negative was being thought. Instead, I would remind myself, *If I have been looking at people and loving their outfits for so long and never telling them, maybe they are doing that too!* I looked at every single person who caught my eye while looking at me, and I smiled! You know what? They smiled back. This very effortless act brought on a new way to project the Karma Clause and potentially change the world around me. The powerful message: lead by example.

That truly is the power that we women hold. We can uplift the world by choosing to uplift others, and in turn, lift up ourselves as well. In business and professional empowerment conversations I heard the saying "A rising tide raises all boats." And it really is so true. If women as a whole adopt a mentality of supporting each other and raising each other up, even if it is through just a simple and random compliment to a stranger on the street, imagine the impact that can have as it spreads across our streets, towns, cities, and states. We can be the rising tide, and together we can lift all the boats.

As a personal stylist, I have found this technique of empowering women to be a way to create a culture of community for women. One that sustains us, encourages us, and secures us. We are all human, and we all have faults, and we all have what makes us fabulous too. Those differences are valuable and important and have a purpose in the world. The more women lift each other up, the stronger we get, and the stronger we get, the easier it is to move mountains together! The Karma Clause is meant to be a catalyst. To start small and continue to multiply exponentially! And it starts with you. Now. Your open heart, your open mind, and your selflessness to say to a stranger, "Wow! I love what you are wearing." You make their day, you uplift your day, and then let the energy domino from there.

Set that example, and you will inspire others to do the same. By doing so, you've become a catalyst for good in this world.

so, let's recap!

- Try catching yourself using the evil eye as you carry on throughout your day, and you will begin to break the habit. Then, notice what you are saying about yourself as you pass people on the street. Your value is not determined by anyone else but you. When you understand we are all equal, you begin to see inspiration and possibility.

- The Karma Clause is the ultimate feel-better-and-make-the-world-a-brighter-place tool. Share your genuine compliments and watch as you change someone's day for the better, all while making yourself feel good in the process. Let that feeling continue to manifest from person to person.

- Having an open heart to others and their personal journeys will make you more compassionate, support more women, and create a community of kindness.

- Set the example in your circles by lifting others up instead of tearing them down. You will inspire others as well as continue to inspire yourself. A rising tide lifts all boats.

style statement

I set the example and lead the way by **lifting** up other women, inspiring women to **lead** with love, and putting positive energy back into the world. Empowering others empowers me.

CHAPTER 11

a life that shines

CHOOSE TO BE HAPPY

On the eve of my thirty-fifth birthday, I was boarding a flight to Paris. I had not taken a vacation for the past six years, let alone traveled to Europe alone before. I'll always remember the moment I walked onto the plane. It was a big moment in my life. It was the moment that everything changed.

A month prior, I had hit a wall in my life. I was actually on the verge of giving up my styling business and going to look for a job. I had been working, hustling, growing, and evolving for six straight years without a break. Living my life that way caused me to feel unhappy, uninspired, entirely lost in my direction, and ready to give up everything I had worked for so far. Additionally, my once successful styling business had become stagnant—well, more like it came to a dead halt. I was rounding out a five-month dry spell without any new business. I had spun my wheels for months trying to get something to spark, starting a million different projects, spreading myself thin, constantly on the hustle for work. Drained and exhausted, I knew my mission was to be an empowering force for women. But because I was so determined to give—giving all my empowered energy away—I never paused to fill up my own energy well. Running on empty, I just kept moving.

I put so much love, time, effort, and energy into my styling business. I had been fortunate enough to be named a top personal stylist in multiple publications, as well as featured in over thirty print and online publications. People knew my name! I had a roster of previous clients who filled my life with joy, and I had an ever-supportive family to stand by my side no matter what. Yet, with all this success, I didn't feel successful at all.

I had worked so hard and come so far, yet there I was, six years into manifesting my dream business, and I felt utterly stuck. I couldn't see through the scarcity mindset I was living in. My lack of clients, lack of money, lack of help. If only I could equate success to all the love and passion I had put into my business. It defeated me. Actually, I defeated myself. So much so, I couldn't even fathom how on earth I would muster the hustle to push through. In my mind, more hustle was the only answer to solve this. And with nothing left to give, giving up sounded like the best option.

Feeling unsuccessful in business permeated into the rest of my life as I also began to feel extremely unsuccessful in love and life enjoyment. At the age of thirty-five, I was still painfully single. Wasn't I supposed to have it all by now? Never in my life would I have expected to be the age I was and still single, with no boyfriend even in sight.

It felt like the clock was a ticking time bomb, and I was watching life fly right by, missing me entirely. I felt that I had been knocked down so many times, by work, by people, by men, I couldn't even get back up again. When I looked back at my life, I kept playing the same broken record of thoughts: *Where did it go? What do I have to show for myself? What is even my purpose anymore?*

They say you have to break down to break through. But for whatever reason, when you are in the middle of a breakdown, that breaking-through part always feels lost in the mix. *How am I going to break through?* I just wanted to run away. *Where can I go?* And it hit me like a bolt of electricity: *Paris.*

"I want to wake up on my thirty-fifth birthday in Paris," is what came out of my mouth that afternoon. In my life, I had never said anything like this to myself; it never even occurred to me to travel or to take a vacation while I was building my business. I had only a few thousand dollars of savings left in the bank, a credit card debt to make me cringe, and no spendable income otherwise. But for the first time in years I decided to follow my heart and not my head. I took all the money I had left and booked a trip to Paris so that I would land at Charles De Gaulle airport on the morning of my thirty-fifth birthday. I literally had nothing left to lose. Putting heart and soul first, ahead of everything else that physically and mentally ailed, was a foreign feeling. It was almost as if my life were spinning out of control and the universe was like, *You need to take the reins, girlfriend.* I did just that.

I can clearly remember walking off the plane and feeling the crisp, fresh air. I was in Paris! I did it! That in itself felt like such an accomplishment. But then I took to the streets to live life, delighted by every little thing I saw and experienced. Parisian fashion! Sidewalk seating and eating oysters with a glass of rosé! The historic buildings juxtaposed with modern street graffiti. The baguettes! The cheese! The butter! The shopping! The champagne! I took a million selfies, and it all felt so fabulous. I felt fabulous. It was the first time I had felt free. Free in my body, mind, and soul. And this was just day one.

At the end of my fabulous first day in Paris, I popped into one last store before heading out to dinner. I wanted to buy myself something special. It was my birthday after all! Cue the record screech. Time stopped, and I noticed a spotlight flicker over a simple gray cropped tank top in direct glowing light. (It was clearly just the bad florescent track lighting of the store, but I took it as a sign of the universe's intervention.) Printed across the chest line of the top was, "I have decided to be happy." And it hit me.

HELLO, LAURIE!

WAKE UP!

THIS IS *YOUR* LIFE!

YOU CAN *CHOOSE* TO BE HAPPY.

My mind was blown from the depth of this concept as well as its simplicity. Life *was* changing, but life wasn't passing me by—**I was letting life pass me by**. Going to Paris was my first attempt to grab on to that passing life train before it was too late.

Paris was all around an eye-opening experience, and the idea of choosing my happiness sank in deeper. I learned on this trip that I truly am sovereign in designing my life. And whatever choices I make—right or wrong—are the correct steps to take. You never know what magic can happen by taking a wrong turn, but if you never make a move either way, then you'll never know in the first place. Every step you do make is the right step, even if leads you down an entirely unexpected path or to a learning experience that you could never have fathomed. Those moments fill your soul.

And my soul was full. For all the wrong turns I made traveling alone, and the perfectly right moments that made my trip so special, I lived out a dream of mine. I made a life-long friend, did a photoshoot at the Eiffel Tower, ate the most delicious macaroons, and experienced myself and my life with wide-open eyes. I was inspired!

Leaving Paris, I was filled with many mixed emotions. I was strong and proud about what I had accomplished for myself, and at the same time, I was terrified to go home and face the reality of my life again. Would I just slip back into my old pattern? Would I be able to choose my happy? Would

I survive this roller coaster I was on? Then, like a jolt of electricity—well, actually with a literal jolt of electricity—the universe made herself known once again.

While sitting at the airport, adjusting my phone cord at a plug between the chairs, an electric shock came charging through my arms, to my heart, and down to my feet. I leapt out of my seat and screamed. I'll never forget that feeling as electricity traveled through my body. I was in sheer and literal shock! And it hurt! My body was vibrating. I was jolted to the core.

A woman sitting two seats away from me looked over and said to me, "You look shocked!" not knowing what had happened yet. I just burst into tears! I couldn't stop crying. She reached over the connected chairs, put her hand gently on my upper arm, looked me in the eye, and said in a calm yet strong and loving voice, "I am here with you. You are going to be okay." (No joke, I'm tearing up as I write this.)

An angel had appeared in my life at the exact time I needed somebody. I had felt so alone and helpless, as if all my empowered feelings had been zapped away with one big shock. But this beautiful soul and stranger, who, believe it or not, was a minister, became a sign from God. She gave me the grace of her soul and soothed that jolt of electricity with love and compassion—something I so rarely gave to myself. We talked for hours as our flight was delayed. She was there for me in a way that not only touched my heart, but it also healed my own soul. Everything was going to be okay. I was going to be okay.

Who we are is a compilation of the stories that got us to where we are today mixed with our big, beautiful vision for our future. What I discovered is that, no matter what your story is, no matter what your life experiences have been, the choices you made and the choices you didn't make, the future is still ahead of you. Your story is still being written. And you can let life write that story for you, or you can pick up the pen and write the story for yourself. You can choose your happiness! You can choose the inspired destiny you want to fulfill. You have the reins! Put on an empowering outfit and take strides forward in the direction that calls to you, the direction that makes you happy.

That direction for me was to pump the brakes a bit on my life and re-center my focus, not on work, but on me. My soul and my self-preservation became my top priority. I made space in my life for me. I found myself taking yoga consistently and journeying within to find my deepest answers and soul callings. I styled myself even more seriously! I wanted to show the world who I truly was. And I couldn't wait to express myself with this new feeling I had bursting from inside. Wearing and embracing all the unique pieces I picked up in Paris, my style became a constant reminder of my own journey to empowerment.

I stopped worrying about what wasn't happening for me and started just enjoying what I did have around me. I made more plans with friends, I went to more events, I connected with new inspiring women who lit up my life, and, most importantly, I put myself back out into the world. I wasn't going to let life pass me by anymore. I was going to live out the life that I dreamed of living. And with that, I did the most empowering thing I could do. I decided to let go. I surrendered to it all. I knew that everything was going to be okay. My airport angel told me so. What I now understand is that when I try to control it all, I lose control of it all. But by letting go of my control and surrendering what I couldn't change to a higher source, I watched as the world blossomed around me as I took action toward my dream life. Eventually, I blossomed too.

Gratitude became my mantra, and choosing my happiness everyday became my credo. I had so many blessings, and the more I saw the beauty in those simple blessings right in front of me, the more blessings started to appear around me. I found myself in a place of love for and acceptance of who I am and where I am in my life, and having a release of the pressure of where I was going. The future was yet to be written, but I was fulfilled, now. I found my happy within myself. Choosing one's own happiness became my new definition of success.

And that success energy permeated everything in my life. In the next six months after returning to Los Angeles, I landed my first major contract as a style ambassador and spokeswoman, which has been my most fulfilling job as a stylist to date. And then on one fated night, I walked into a dive bar, overdressed and unattached, and there he was: my future husband. We met, we fell in love, we married and had a baby. Life couldn't be grander.

POSSIBILITY IN EVERY OPPORTUNITY

Traveling solo to Paris opened my eyes to the way I was experiencing my life. Correction: to the way I *wasn't* experiencing my life. I was so laser-focused for so long on the minutiae in my day-to-day life that I was neglecting to step outside myself and see the world around me. That is what Paris truly did. It took me out of my life and let me float from above and all around to see that the world is so much bigger than only what I could focus on. The world has so much more to offer. The world is filled with inspiration and so much possibility! It was at that moment I knew I had to change how I saw the immediate world around me.

Have you ever held your hands up to your eyes to make pretend binoculars? All you can see is what is in front of you. All you can focus on is what is right there through the "lenses." Try it right now: make your hand binoculars, and keep your hands there for at least sixty seconds. Take a look at the book font; take a look around the room you're in. Walk around a bit. *Don't trip!* See the world around you with your vision focused and your peripheral view blocked.

After the minute or so release your hands, and what do you see? You see that the world around you is much bigger and brighter when you can see the whole picture. I look at life in this manner too. When you get so caught up in your personal life, you sometimes can focus on only the microscopic details of what is in front of you. Everything you are experiencing seems like such a big deal! But! The world around you is much brighter and filled with possibility if only you take off your personal blinders and open your eyes to really see the *whole* world around you.

The idea of choosing to be happy means choosing to see opportunity at every turn and believing in the possibility of that. How exhilarating! It is choosing to *live* life as it comes your way and to navigate those sometimes rocky roads with an open heart and an open mind, knowing that if you can stay above the madness, you can get through it.

Shifting your perspective to see possibility is a very powerful tool. How many times through the process of this book did you say, "I didn't think I could do that!"? But then you tried it out for yourself and discovered that it works for you too! And, bonus, you liked it! This is why I wanted you to throw out all your fashion rules from the get-go. They don't just hold us back when *dressing* our best selves, they hold us back from *being* our best selves. When you discover your unique way to style and self-expression, which you once felt to be impossible and therefore stopped yourself before even trying, everything then begs the question, If what you once thought was impossible *is* possible, what else is possible in your life? Is that *one* thing you've been telling yourself for years is impossible actually possible? It absolutely is! You just have to go for it.

Perhaps it's putting your hat in the ring for the next-level-up job. Or maybe it's meeting "the one." Or what about breaking off from your nine-to-five to start your own business? Or maybe you are like me and you just need to let go and start living your life feeling fulfilled and untethered from your own baggage. All those things are entirely up to you, and the simple act of exploring your wardrobe to design and own a style that represents the total *you* is your personal catalyst for creation! By living with a new mindset, embracing a fresh attitude about you and what you are a capable of, surrendering to what you can't change, yet opening your eyes to all the possibilities that surround you, all you can do is create your own magic.

The experience with style in the morning is the first opportunity to pause in a busy life. In that space, you have an opportunity to acknowledge where you are at that current moment and then use your wardrobe to empower you throughout your day. When you show up for yourself, you are not just showing up for you, you are also setting the stage for your day ahead, all the while inspiring others to do the same. Create that kind of energy around you and the opportunities you can manifest are limitless. The Law of Attraction is on our side! Too many times, our eyes are clouded as we walk through our lives or our invisible binoculars get locked onto a focused space. Getting dressed is your defiance of a monotonous, unfulfilled life. No matter what your life is, choose to master every morning with this style mindset, dress for your highest self, and you win every day.

STYLE ALIGNMENT

When we hear the word *surrender* it's easy to assume that means to give up. But *surrender*, like *style*, has a deeper, more soul-centered meaning. Surrendering is letting go of what you fear the most: the unknown. It is releasing yourself from what holds you back, unbinding yourself from what holds you in, and untethering yourself from what holds you down. We all get so mentally tangled up in our lives, our stories, our pasts, our futures, and our closets! Surrendering is liberation. And when we are liberated, we are free to be the master of our own destinies.

Am I a broken record yet? *Style* is so much more than the clothing. And Stylepowerment is so much more than just feeling motivated and energetic when getting dressed. I am talking about heart-centered style and fully embodied self-expression. I call this Style Alignment, which comes from fully stepping into who you are—mind, body, soul, and style. As you tear down your barriers, break your patterns, and rise above the limiting beliefs that hold you back, you begin to expand, growing brighter and brighter. When we live consciously like this, in all areas of our lives, we begin to see how much fuller life and our lives can be. Getting dressed adds to your personal enjoyment and fulfillment of life. And when we feel that good, no matter what our lives are, our jobs are, or our challenges, we are reminded that we are capable of overcoming what lies ahead.

So how do we release ourselves from the tangled webs of our minds? We must get back into our bodies. You know that feeling when you start shaking your hips and moving your body to your favorite song? The mind stops thinking and the body takes over with your personal expression. Getting back into your body is another magical aspect to your style. When you dance and move, your conscious mind allows your body to take the wheel and just feel. Feel the music, feel the movement, feel your body. That feeling is embodiment. It is the acknowledgment and ownership of the skin you are in.

But what about embodyment? (And yes, I know it's spelled wrong, but the word *body* is a vital part of the intended meaning here.) *Embodiment* is feeling *you* in your skin. Style em*body*ment is feeling *you*, deeply, in your clothes. It is feeling your true self, your heart-center and your inner energy, physically in your body. Style Alignment! When you wear an outfit that flatters your figure, makes you feel good, and supports your confidence, you are essentially embodying YOU. How can you not feel amazing? Like dancing it out, wearing your clothes in an empowering way helps you embody the woman you are. The more often you dress yourself to be your best *you*, the more you will continue to embody your best *you*! Remember, she's already in there; she's just waiting for her moment to shine!

Self-expression plays a big part in your personal embodyment too. Self-expression is revealing *you* in your clothes. What you put on your body can reveal all the beautiful aspects about you, and as we've covered in this book, you can use wardrobe to send off those messages however you see fit! By showing your true *you* to the world, you electrify your personal magnetism. Self-expression is owning the multifaceted *you*, then utilizing that self-acceptance to style yourself in a way that shows off your inspiring story. Self-expression in your style is a declaration to the world.

When we master our own empowered embodyment and personal self-expression, the feeling of freedom comes to mind. When you release yourself from what holds you back, there is only one way to go from there: forward into a future you can actively choose to design. Freedom, from a style perspective, is ultimately the true essence of style. *Freedom* is liberating yourself from attachment to the past and fear of the unknown and allowing yourself to explore, create, and *be* in any way that you design. And that liberation is exactly the purpose of this book. To release you from what holds you back and to give you permission to make the future and your style whatever you want it to be. Your destiny is up to you. Your expression is up to you. Your life is up to you. **YOU are the style!** And your style is your own manifestation of your future. Letting go enables you to style freely and creatively without fear so that the world can see the magnificent you.

True embodied *style* is freedom self-expressed. Embracing yourself and your style is liberation from the mental blocks that stop you from putting on something that could be life changing! All those times you halted and said, "No, I can't do that," will be replaced with "WHY NOT?! Let's try it and see!" It's that kind of open mentality and mindset about yourself, your style, and *your life* that allow magical possibilities to enter your life. Why? Because your eyes are wide-open to see it! Each morning you are giving yourself time to be with yourself, to be present, to be intentional, and to be creative and have a little fun. This is what creating space for yourself looks like. You are taking each day as another chance to make a difference for you. Most importantly, you are putting together daily outfits align with who you are and that illuminate your shine as you go take on the world. You are designing your life with every outfit.

SHINE BRIGHT LIKE A DIAMOND

Life is a wild ride, full of ups and downs, left turns and right turns, even roller-coaster-like at times. One thing remains throughout it all. *You.* And no matter what life throws your way, you are still the master of your own destiny. Not only can you choose your happy, by wearing a wardrobe that feels like your most embodied *you*, you stay connected to yourself and your heart-center at any point in time in your life. No matter what curve-balls life may throw, you can always make a choice to show up every day for yourself, put on an outfit that makes you feel spectacular, and take on your day like the dynamic, unique, powerful woman that you are.

Your style is your choice, and your choice is entirely up to you. It's your

own story to share, reshape, and redesign again and again. Life may change, you will change, we all evolve and age, but through it all, getting dressed each day to show the world your brilliance is something that will always remain. You have to get dressed! And each morning is a new opportunity to start over and show the world what you've got. You control the narrative of your style story, always. With all the twists and turns that life has to offer, you now have something solid to consistently come back to: your style, your self-expression, and your powerful freedom to do so!

I have always believed that the experience and expression of style can fuel the core of our inner strength and empowerment. That is the essence of Stylepowerment—the use of style to empower your life at any point in time. To boost you when you are low, to give you that gusto when you need more strength, and to push you higher when you are at the brink of a big leap. Style is your ever-evolving and creative companion that will always be there for you as you take each day on. How you feel each day can have a direct effect on how you reveal yourself through your wardrobe. Fight those negative feelings (as they *will* come to challenge you) by styling your most confident look regardless of how you feel. Do that and you win every time.

Your style is the true key to not only living your most desired life but to expressing your ownership of your whole self, which shines beyond your body. We all know that amazing things come not just from manifestation and prayer but from hard work toward our goals too. Getting dressed each morning and choosing you *is* hard work. Style is your ultimate tool to putting yourself out into the world in a way that stands out, steps up, and makes a statement on your behalf. And as you know, it will also lift your mood, raise your vibration, and create magnetism in your life. Style has power you can harness to shine throughout your whole life experience! All you have to do is get up and get dressed.

so, let's recap!

- Choose to be happy! Your experience in life, like your personal style, is a choice! Choose your happiness no matter what the universe throws in your direction. Finding peace, contentment, and joy in any situation will always lead you toward the light.

- There is truly possibility in every opportunity. We have to open our eyes, minds, and hearts to the big, bright world around us. Getting outside of yourself can be just the medicine your heart needs to see your world with a wider vision.

- Your Style Alignment is where your Self and freedom of expression meet. You can do and be anything you want to be! Let your wardrobe support that feeling of embodiment, and support the style story you want to put out into the world.

- Stylepowerment is your secret weapon to manifestation. By utilizing your personal expression as you get dressed, you are sending your positive and intentional vibrations out into the world for the universe to take in and send back your way. Start every day with an outfit that makes you feel like your highest self, and you will shine bright like a diamond.

As I write these last words for the book I have always dreamed of writing, I have to leave you with a final thought of what I care about the most. I care about you. I care about your well-being. I care about your happiness. I care about your confidence. I care about your success. I care about your voice being heard. I care about you being seen. I care about you being taken seriously. I care about how you love yourself. I care about how treat your body. I care about how you feel every day and then express that in your wardrobe.

You have the power to do, be, and achieve anything! You have the magic inside to shine from the inside out. It requires getting dressed with intention; honoring your true self; strengthening your confidence daily through creative self-expression, radical self-love, and acceptance; total embodiment; and a sense of how you truly shine. You got this, girl! You have the power to break through. You have the power to step up! You have the ability to show up. And it is your destiny to do so! You are the master of that destiny.

So, how will you use your power?

Go put on an outfit that makes you feel confident, beautiful, sexy, magnetic, energetic, powerful, and perfectly you. Keep your waist definition high, your head held higher, your spirits to the limitless sky, and your vision toward that bright, shining, inspired life you get to create each day. You are entirely heart-open and full of possibility. You are already amazing! Now go show the whole world who you are.

style statement

I am the style!

CPSIA information can be obtained
at www.ICGtesting.com
Printed in the USA
LVHW061354020821
694319LV00009B/297